African Magic Series

HAITIAN VODOU

MONIQUE JOINER SIEDLAK

Oshun
Publications

Haitian Vodou © 2019 Monique Joiner Siedlak

All rights reserved. This book or parts thereof may not be reproduced in any form, stored in any retrieval system, or transmitted in any form by any means—electronic, mechanical, photocopy, recording, or otherwise—without prior written permission of the publisher, except as provided by United States of America copyright law.

Under no circumstances will any blame or legal responsibility be held against the publisher, or author, for any damages, reparation, or monetary loss due to the information contained within this book. Either directly or indirectly.

ISBN-13: 978-1-948834-99-5

Publisher

Oshun Publications, LLC

Legal Notice:

This book is copyright protected. This book is only for personal use. You cannot amend, distribute, sell, use, quote or paraphrase any part, or the content within this book, without the consent of the author or publisher.

Disclaimer Notice:

Please note the information contained within this document is for educational and entertainment purposes only. All effort has been executed to present accurate, up to date, and reliable, complete information. No warranties of any kind are declared or implied. Readers acknowledge that the author is not engaging in the rendering of legal, financial, medical or professional advice. The content within this book has been derived from various sources. Please consult a licensed professional before attempting any techniques outlined in this book.

By reading this document, the reader agrees that under no circumstances is the author responsible for any losses, direct or indirect, which are incurred as a result of the use of information contained within this document, including, but not limited to, — errors, omissions, or inaccuracies.

Cover Design by MJS

Cover Image by Depositphotos.com

Other Books in the Series

African Spirituality Beliefs and Practices
Hoodoo
Seven African Powers: The Orishas
Cooking For the Orishas
Lucumi: The Ways of Santeria
Voodoo of Louisiana

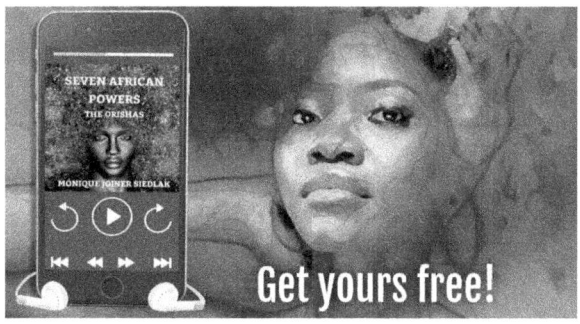

Want to learn about African Magic, Wicca, or even Reiki while cleaning your home, exercising, or driving to work? I know it's tough these days to simply find the time to relax and curl up with a good book. This is why I'm delighted to share that I have books available in audiobook format.

Best of all, you can get the audiobook version of this book or any other book by me for free as part of a 30-day Audible trial.

Members get free audiobooks every month and exclusive discounts. It's an excellent way to explore and determine if audiobook learning works for you.

If you're not satisfied, you can cancel anytime within the trial period. You won't be charged, and you can still keep your book. To choose your free audiobook, visit:

www.mojosiedlak.com/free-audiobooks

Contents

Introduction — xi

1. What Exactly is Haitian Vodou? — 1
2. The Lwa — 11
3. Vodou in Haiti Today — 53
4. Haitian Vodou Ceremonies and Rites of Passage — 55
5. First Steps in Haitian Vodou — 63
6. Magic and Sorcery — 73

Conclusion — 77
Glossary — 79
About the Author — 85
More Books by Monique Joiner Siedlak — 87
Please Review — 89

Introduction

I am glad and thankful that you chose this book to learn more about the intriguing ways of Vodou and its history in Haiti. There is so much to the culture of Haiti, and I am looking forward to our journey together as we explore the realm of Vodou in Haiti.

Haiti is a country that is surrounded by local beauty, mystery, and intrigue. Their history is colorful, tragic, and a story that is not known enough by people around the world. Haiti did not always have that name, in fact, when it was first found by English colonizers, Haiti was called Hispaniola, otherwise known as little Spain.

The significance of Haiti in our history is that it was one of the primary gateways into what is now known as the Caribbean. It was a prosperous area in 1492, but closer towards the sixteenth century when the new world was coming around, Santo Domingo as it was later known, lost its prominence and fell to ruin. Thanks to the French interests in the latter part of the eighteenth century, Santo Domingo (or Saint-Domingue as the French renamed it) reclaimed its prominence in the area.

Despite its beautiful terrain and its importance to colonizers of the time, Haiti had a troubled past. It was embroiled in the

Introduction

middle of a battle with slavery, with over five hundred thousand of its residents being slaves. Why was slavery so important? Well, it was the labor force that saw Haiti rise into the glory that it had acquired.

With so many of Haiti's slaves coming over from Africa, their beliefs came too and were formed into a religion. There is so much to Haiti's culture that was impacted both by the slave trade in the New World and the forced religion of Roman Catholicism on those who lived within Haiti's shores.

The slaves of the past created a religion in Vodou that would become a sanctuary and a way of life for many people in Haiti, including for many today. Even once Haiti was a free nation, the religion had grown so much that it was a part of who the people in Haiti were.

Haiti had still experienced tumult since the days of slavery, especially when just recently, they suffered the effects of a devastating earthquake. But the spirit of the people of Haiti is strong. Through this book, we are going to explore a vital aspect of where the people of Haiti form their beliefs and how Vodou helps keep them going.

ONE

What Exactly is Haitian Vodou?

The official religion in Haiti is Roman Catholicism, which it has been since the times of slavery. In spite of that, Vodou is still considered a prominent religion in Haiti, and today is widely used and believed in by the people of Haiti. In fact, studies have determined that the majority of Haitians practice or at least find in some of the rituals and belief systems of Vodou. Unlike other religions where they are the only one, a lot of Vodouists believe that Vodou and Roman Catholicism can co-exist together. So, rather than fight against Catholicism, they embrace it with their Vodou beliefs.

With the way that misinformation spreads and grows a lot of misconceptions have been borne about what Vodou really is. There have been a lot of blunt individuals who have given Haiti the reputation of sorcery for their practices in Vodou. But these rumors and images should be taken with a massive grain of salt because they do not depict how Vodou really works.

Vodou is based on family spirits. As I mentioned above, those who practice and believe in Vodou also believe in Roman Catholicism. Many Vodou practitioners also claim to be Roman Catholics. Funnily enough, if you grew up in Haiti, the word Vodou might even be a foreign concept to you or at least the meaning behind the word. In rural Haiti, there is no word for Vodou in their language system.

The relationship between Roman Catholicism and Vodou is an interesting one, especially as most see their belief in the spirits as merely serving the spirits and not as a separate belief or religious system. Vodou falls into multiple categories in Haiti: there is the service to the family spirits (we will learn more about this soon) and then the practice of magic and sorcery.

Vodou is a belief system that revolves around spirits that are categorized into families. These spirits are commonly called Lwa. You cannot just pick and choose which spirits to serve as they are inherited based on your ancestor's lineage. The purpose of the Lwa is to protect their family from harm and misfortune, and so in return, the families that are protected serve the Lwa with offerings of food and other small gifts.

There are also specific services that can be held to serve and strengthen the familial bonds between the family and the Lwa. There is an annual service that occurs where a ceremony and ritual are dedicated to the Lwa, and then there is another type of ritual that happens much less frequently. Usually, this second ritual only occurs once within a generation, mainly because having this ritual is expensive. The families that are on harder times might elect to perform this ceremony only when they need their family bonds strengthened with their Lwa spirits.

The spirits of the Lwa are plentiful in the realm of Vodou, and they are separated into several different families. Three main groups of Lwa are observed in the Haiti Region: the Rada, the Petro, and the Gede. We will explore each family throughout this introduction to Haitian Vodou. It is important to note that with the Rada Lwa they tend to be softer and sweeter spirits, while Petro Lwa are often said to be stricter as they demand more and expect more from their children and descendants. Rada Lwa also hails from African origins while most of the Petro Lwa originated from Haiti.

The Lwa you will learn about have their own distinct

personalities and identities. Most Lwa are kindred spirits, but you can get some malevolent or mischievous family members in there as well. When you displease a Lwa, their most common method of retribution is to ignore you or make you fall ill. The Lwa can also mess up your material possessions and standings in life. Remember that your family's Lwa is the only Lwa that you can serve, and that will help you because other Lwa have no obligation to you.

The most straightforward means of interacting with the family spirits is through visions and dreams. The Lwa will appear to you and speak to you through symbols or direct verbalization in your dreams. There is also the belief that the Lwa can possess control over bodies. The possession puts the person typically in a trance-like state, and others will notice their traits changing to take on those represented by the Lwa spirit possessing them.

Frequently possession only happens when a ritual is performed in service to a specific Lwa. Sometimes it can occur when a dance to honor the Lwa is going on as well. A Lwa that takes possession does not do so out of malice but rather to bring warning or even to explain events to its family. The Lwa can also interact with those around it during this time and flirt, laugh or even bring out the truth about deeds that were hidden by a member.

There are more than just the Lwa spirits in Vodou history; having said that, the other entities that are a component of this vibrant religion are the ancestors. The ancestors are the dead, and there are often elaborate ceremonies performed to honor the dead and their role in our world. If you travel through Haiti, you might notice that they have beautiful tombs that are built for their dead, and this is merely illustrating how important their dead are to them. It is said that like the Lwa, the dead ancestors can appear in dreams with warnings of tidings that are to come. Those who practice Vodou exchange their servings to the Lwa for things, such as material wealth or even protection and in some cases, vengeance.

Through this book, you will read about the Houngan and the mambo. These are simply the male and female names for Vodou specialists—priests and priestesses. They are the bridge for mediation between humans and spirits. They are considered to be wise and knowledgeable in the art of Vodou and should be skilled at performing rituals and using herbal remedies for their people.

Where Roman Catholicism has an organized level of hierarchy in its belief system, Vodou has none of that. Some Houngans and Mambos will create stronger relationships with certain Lwa, but there is no indicated level to which Lwa is better than the one before.

History of Vodou in Haiti

As mentioned before, Haiti has a startling history that is both sad and uplifting. But, what about the history of Vodou in Haiti? To explore this, it is crucial to take an in-depth look at the timeline of events for slavery in Haiti as the two go hand in hand.

In 1750, there were over 500,000 Africans in Haiti (Saint Domingue at the time). These Africans were brought over to Haiti to be slave labor. While there were French colonists in Haiti at this time, they only made up about 40,000 of the population. That is a pretty stark contrast to the amount of Africans that were enslaved in Haiti.

Since the French colonizer's main religion was Catholicism, they forced all of the African slaves to adopt their faith and go through christening. Despite this forced christening, Vodou emerged amongst the slaves as their own beliefs intertwined with the doctrines of the French religion. The beginning of Vodou that emerged was a mix of ancient African religions and the new teachings of Catholicism they were forced to adopt as their own.

Interestingly enough, there were Vodou priests who led

revolts against the colonizers, and the early Vodou priests hailed from Muslim backgrounds. Through these revolts, it became apparent that Vodou would become a platform for resistance against the French; it united the slaves against the colonizers.

In 1751, Makandal escaped from slavery in Haiti and went on to become one of the most famous Vodou leaders of his time. He also led revolts and uprisings against the colonizers. Unfortunately, Makandal was captured, and in 1758, a mere seven years from his escape, he was burned at stake for his practices and beliefs. Because these Vodou priests were standing up to the colonizers, they viewed practicing Vodou as a direct sign of revolt against them. So, as a way to control it, they forbade any other ceremony or ritual that was not Catholic. Another way that they controlled the slaves was to prohibit them from gathering in places if they belonged to different slave owners. Even slave owners separated their Catholic services. If a slave was caught meeting up with a slave from a different master, they were severely whipped and branded with an iron. If they were branded once and found as a second offender, then they were sentenced to death.

It was in 1773 when Saint Domingue (Haiti) became one of the wealthiest economies in the world. It was producing over 100,000 tons of sugar and over 80,000 tons of coffee. It also produced around 2,000 tons of cotton. By the close of the eighteenth century, suddenly the French colony of Haiti was amongst the top exporters of coffee and sugar in the world. In fact, the foundation that would go on to become the French Revolution was laid down by the Haitians and their backbreaking slave work.

In 1779, there was a third group of people who were prominent in Haiti the people of color who were free. These were mostly the children of African mothers and French fathers. In fact, the tides were turning and at least a quarter of the slaves and properties were owned by people of color who were considered free. But race laws were cracking down in the, and by the year 1779, it had become illegal for even those people of color who were free to emulate the style of white colonizers.

As a direct result, the tension came to a head in 1790 when the free people of color decided to an uprising against those who would oppress them. It culminated in one man, Vincent Ogé, who summoned hundreds of free people of color to stage a revolt. Unfortunately, his rebellion failed, and he, along with nineteen others, was executed for their actions. But with that failure, the fight for freedom did not stop. It was August of 1791 when another slave revolution came around. Armies of slaves rose up against their colonizers and by the time September had come and gone over 200 sugar plantations and over 1,000 coffee plantations had been destroyed. Thousands of slaves had escaped during this mass revolt as well.

Boukman was a Vodou priest who had stood up and organized this revolt successfully. Through secret Vodou gatherings, they had planned their course of action. In Vodou history, they say that Boukman created an agreement with the spirits of Haiti. Boukman pledged that he would serve them for 200 years if they helped him free themselves and gain their liberty. While he was at the forefront during the start of the revolution, eventually Boukman was killed in November of 1791.

The battle may have been won, but the war was not so quickly finished. It took many more years of fighting to have people of color regain their liberty. It was in 1804 when Jean-Jacques Dessalines stated that Haiti was free. On January 1st of 1804, it officially became the free Republic of Haiti. It was a momentous occasion in history as it was only the second state to become free in the New World. It was also the only country to have gained its freedom entirely through the liberation of the former slaves.

Despite this freedom, Haiti was boycotted and isolated from the rest of the world as they refused to acknowledge Haiti's independence. Because of this cold front, Haiti's economy suffered severely.

During this time, the leaders who had led the revolt through Vodou practices removed themselves from the association with Vodou. They wanted to conduct themselves as the French colonizers did to be accepted as Frenchman and Catholics. Even though they did not differentiate between the two religions, they wanted the acceptance from the colonizers.

France directed Haiti to pay 150 million francs to renew commerce so that they could retrieve their economy. This was said to be the compensation for all of their lost slaves. Haiti took out a considerable amount of loans to pay the damages to France and dug themselves into a deeper hole.

Still, those who practiced Vodou wanted it to be recognized, but it was going to be a more prolonged battle for this. In 1835, Vodou was outlawed, and anyone found practicing it would be punished. So, secret Vodou societies continued to thrive during this time.

Haiti was still struggling, and by the end of the nineteenth century, a massive 80% of their budget was being spent on loan repayments.

America invaded Haiti in 1915 and occupied it as their own. They took control of everything, including Haiti's national bank. This was in an attempt to guarantee all the repayments of foreign debts. But there was dissent among the locals who did not agree with the invasion, so talk of revolt was steadily growing again. Haiti was occupied by America until 1934, but during this time, Vodou societies grew back. For all that, the presence of the USA repressed the practice of Vodou even more.

Élie Lescot was the president in 1941, and he was supported by the USA. He was a corrupt dictator, and there was a vast war that erupted against Vodou when he was in office. The Houngans and Mambos were imprisoned for their rituals, Vodou temples were destroyed, and artifacts were tossed away like trash. The practitioners of Vodou did not stay silent. Nevertheless, they continued to meet and conduct their rituals in private.

Finally, in 1947, Haiti made the final repayment for the debt they had incurred to France. It was a time where they could start rebuilding. But the economy only got worse, and the poverty level continued to rise steadily.

It was not until the 1950s when a black middle class emerged, and there were more military coups that Vodou began to be more publicly tolerated and accepted. Vodou was finally being studied by people with respect, and a tourist industry grew on the back of the Vodou rituals.

Papa Doc became president of Haiti in 1957. The tyranny of the previous regime was eradicated, and the elite were thrown out. This caused a lot of Haitians who were educated to flee due to their loss of power.

Papa Doc thought that Vodou was a part of Haiti's culture and an essential part of their African heritage. Because of his Vodou knowledge and the increasing popularity of Vodou during his reign, Papa Doc's power also grew.

Unfortunately, Papa Doc grew into a dictator himself, and his regime led to brutally. There were thousands of Haitians who had to flee their country, and even more that were murdered. It was not until 1971 when Jean-Claude Duvalier finally succeeded that the brutal killing finally stopped.

Shortly after this, it was declared free to practice Vodou in Haiti in 1972. For a while, Haiti saw some return to normalcy. But in 1896, a new military coup came into play and removed Duvalier from power. The year 1990 saw a new Catholic priest take the presidency. There was a call for religious freedom during Jean-Bertrand Aristide's presidency, but there continued to be fighting in Haiti. After only holding office for eight months, a military coup overthrew Aristide. Many more Haitian lives were lost in these battles.

The USA invaded again in 1994. They brought demanded changes for the economy of Haiti and forced them to cut duties on their products, which caused them to stop production. Because of the tax relief that major companies received, it hit

Haiti hard, and it was in 1999 that they were reduced to a mere 20% of their former production glory.

Despite UN troops being present in Haiti, there was still a lot of political arrest going into the early 2000s. Because of the USA's interference, more Christian people created movements and have tried to establish their faith in Haiti. These movements created a clear distance between Christianity and Vodou.

Finally, in 2003, Vodou was recognized as an official religion in Haiti.

Today Haiti is recognized as one of the poorest countries in the world, being in the top twenty. The rate of unemployment is really high, and a lot of corruption exists among government officials. Many people are not fed enough, and the status of medical care is so poor that preventable epidemics are frequent. But, the belief in Vodou and the practice of Vodou rituals persist today. Vodou is seen as an art that commands dignity.

The Principles and Ethics of Vodou in Haiti

Vodou holds many different variations of the name. In this book, we use both Voodoo and Vodou. While Vodou is practiced all over the world, it is mainly relevant to the Caribbean, especially Haiti.

Vodou was banned, and there were many restrictions put on the practice and belief in Vodou, but that was when the world was naive about it. Vodou is based mainly on the saints of the Catholic religion. While many people think Vodou is a violent religion, it is actually based on peace and faith.

Vodou's principles are not to harm others but rather to heal and to increase knowledge and understanding of our world.

Controversies About Haiti's Vodou Practices

Today, a lot of misinformation is still spread about Voodoo practices around the world. When people hear the word Voodoo, they automatically associate it with the worship of the devil, torture, evil, powerful magic, and even cannibalism. Thanks to Hollywood and inaccurate information, these images have been hard to disassociate with Voodoo.

The misinformation about Vodou dates far back in time but can be documented as early as 1791 when an incident happened at Bois Caiman. It was when a lot of Haitian slaves were leading uprisings against their owners. But the word spread that some people had seen a Vodou ceremony in which a pact was being made with the devil to win their wars. People still believe that this took place until today and will blame Haiti's current economic state on their pact.

But that is not how Vodou is practiced. During slavery, there were a lot of violent and brutal times, and Vodou did work to bring revolters together and unite them. For all that, the main focus of Vodou is the communication and serving of the family spirits for personal health and gain, not for evil.

TWO

The Lwa

At this time, you should be familiar with the phrases and principles of the Vodou family in Haiti. Haiti's Vodou is more commonly spelled Vodou, and its practices are distinct to its history and culture.

The Lwa are part of a group of three families in the Vodou family. They are classified as supernatural beings. These three groups that exist in Haitian Vodou are les Morts (the ancestors), les Mystere (the Lwa), and les Marassa (the sacred twins). In this chapter, we are going to check out the Lwa further individually and understand their family tree more in-depth.

The same way that there are three main sectors of the Vodou family, there are also three central branches on the family tree of the Vodou family. As mentioned before, they are the "Rada" Lwa, "Petro" Lwa, and the "Gede" Lwa. In essence, the Lwa are deities that are invoked by those who practice Vodou to help channel their powers. Remember that the practices and rituals you partake in depending on what family you want to work with and invoke. They are all connected because they are from the same family, but each family branch will have its own ceremonies.

The Rada Lwa

Remember, when we explored the history of slavery in Haiti in the introduction? That particular aspect is important to pay attention to as we examine the first family branch that is summoned in the Lwa family tree.

The Rada Lwa's origin begins in Africa. They are the spirits that the Africans worshipped and prayed to before they were enslaved and brought to Haiti. Because they were deities that these slaves worshipped, as more of them were forced into a concentrated area for their slave labor, the presence of the Rada Lwa took over in the culture. No longer were they smaller spirits or deities that were called upon, but they became a more prominent feature of the religion that was cultivated by the slaves in the new world.

It is important to note that these spirits are not hateful or unkind and vengeful spirits. Their spirits are associated with the color spectrum with white, and they are known to be gentle and benevolent. This is why they seem to be the first of the Lwa to be called upon by their seekers. Let us examine some of the more popular deities that are part of the Rada Lwa.

Legba

Legba is a spirit of the Lwa who is more commonly referred to as "Papa Legba." He is considered the gatekeeper to the spirits of the Lwa family, and as such is one of the first spirits that are called upon in Vodou ceremonies and rituals. Papa Legba is akin to an authority figure or a regulator as he is the spirit who decides which other deities can pass through the spirit realms and answer the call of the Vodou. He is said to guard the Poto Mitan, which is where the spirits are kept and to access the other spirits, one must first serve Papa Legba for he is the bridge of communication for humanity and the essence of the Lwa.

The spirit of Papa Legba can be deceiving to those who do not understand his real power, for he appears to you as an older man who is gentle and handicapped. His clothes are not grand, but rather more suited for a poor man and he walks with a limp. His appearance does deceive many, but for those who know about the "gatekeeper," they know that he is one of the most dominant Lwa in the spiritual realm.

He can take possession of a mortal body and command their words and actions, which is the sign of a powerful deity. He is called upon often in the Rada rites and ceremonies to gain access to other spirits that can help and protect them, but he is not afraid to ask for compensation for his gatekeeping services. Often Papa Legba is distinguishable in the Vodou religion by his sack that is made from straw—it is called a "djakout." This sack carries the offerings and payments that have been made to him in exchange for his help.

Papa Legba is not a lonely spirit, and in the history of Vodou, he is married. Adjessi is Legba's wife, and she is a great support to him, often helping Legba with his tasks or duties.

Legba is known as a powerful Lwa and gatekeeper. Because of his duties, he is often also called a wanderer since he frequently travels back and forth to answer the calls of those who call upon him in ceremonies. During the ritualistic dances in ceremonies, some specific salutes and movements must be performed to give honor to Legba.

While Legba is a generous and benevolent spirit, which does not mean that he does not have a funny side. There are times where he will play tricks on those who summon him. If he feels like he has been slighted or has not been paid enough, he will see it fit to take away that which you value in life. When you make requests of Legba, it is said that you should be very careful in the wording of what you are asking for because he may grant you what you are seeking but in the funniest or unfortunate way. If you are trying to summon Legba through Rada rites, it is advised you do not do this alone and use someone who is experienced in Haitian Vodou.

The Marassa

I know you may possibly be a little confused right now since you read that the Marassa make up their own branch of the Lwa family. Bear with me as we go through the history of this

Vodou. The Marassa can be their own branch because they can be called upon and paid homage to in more than one ceremony. They are found in both Rada rites and Petro rites.

Their common name is the sacred twins. This is how they are known to those who practice Vodou, and they manifest in many different ways. The idea of calling upon the sacred twins is so that we can have what we are seeking come to us twofold or more. Simply because they are the sacred twins does not limit them to the number two, but instead, they can manifest in many different quantities.

Many images represent or symbolize the Marassa Deux (divine twins). But for all that, they are more commonly seen as young twin boys. In fact, the Marassa appear in many different forms and are named differently for each figure they take on. Besides the Marassa Deux, you also have the Marassa Twa (divine triplets). The Marassa Twa are represented as three young girls who are often accompanying Papa Marassa, and they stay around or near his feet. The Marassa Twa are called Faith, Hope, and Charity.

The Marassa are not relegated to just one rite, but both the Rada rituals and Petro rituals can call on the spirits of the Marassa. Each ceremony, at any rate, uses different colors for their serving. The Rada colors are green and yellow while the Petro colors manifest in reds and greens.

The Marassa represent the mysteries of the divine. This is why, in Haitian belief, the Marassa twins are sacred. Those in Haitian culture who have given birth to twins are considered extremely lucky and are honored in Haiti. The honorary names that are given to them are "Manman Gimo" and "Papa Gimo." The names simply translate to Mama and Papa Marassa. Because the twins that are born are a symbol that represents luck, the sacred they are the more they are invited to many events and into people's private homes.

The spirit of the Marassa will never appear as anything else than children, and when they possess someone, they will often take on many child-like personality traits. They do prefer to be around other children because they are still children. Despite their appearance as children, they are still spirits that should not be underestimated. Their power is immense, and they have great wisdom and knowledge concerning the world. The Marassa are also known as healers, and Haitians often call upon them to help heal those in need.

In Haitian culture, there is a need to serve the Marassa with an offering, particularly if you wish to call upon them. For the Rada, you will give them an offering on Thursdays, but the Petro rites serve the Marassa on Tuesday. Another option is to serve them their offering on Saturday. When you serve them, you have several options, but the most popular is to put candy, popcorn, peanuts, fruity drinks, and even cookies on a woven platter for them. If you do not have woven platters, a more straightforward offering is done by making use of two or more pots made from earthenware. These pots are supposed to be part of a system called a "criche" in which they are connected to clay cups as well. The pots are filled with water, and the cups or dishes at the bottom of the pots are filled with offerings such as popcorn.

Remember that the Marassa are child-like spirits, so in your offerings to them focus it on what children would like. Small marbles and toys will also work. Do not separate their offerings or give one more than the other, because they are twins and as such what you place in the offering for the one you must do so in the offering for another. The most important aspect is to enjoy serving the Marassa and have fun with it. They might be ancient spirits, yet their nature is playful as is with any child. Do not approach them with heavy hearts, but rather with smiles and joy.

Because the Marassa are representations of the divine mystery, there is still a great deal of information about them that the world will never know. It is just important to follow the traditions that are known to work when communicating with the Marassa.

Loko and Ayizan

Loko and Ayizan are spirits that are said to be married to one another. That said, before we look at how they interact together, let us take a look at each deity separately. Ayizan Velekete is her full name, which means "chosen friend of the earth." Ayizan is particularly crucial in the realm of Vodou as she is the first priestess (known as Mambo in Vodou culture). Ayizan tends to show up during Vodou initiation rituals. These rituals are called Kanzo Ceremonies.

Ayizan's appearance is similar to that of a woman who sells wares at the market. She wears a white dress with pockets filled to the brim with candy. This candy is then handed out to the children that encounter her. Her appearance is not that of a young woman either but of an older woman. When representing her in symbolism, you show her as small hills of the Earth that you anoint with oil and place palm fringes around the Earth.

Since Ayizan is one of the oldest spirits of Vodou, it is only right that she is served offerings before others. Ayizan is gentle and quiet, though, and while she does not often possess people, she is non-violent when she does. In fact, a person that has been possessed by the spirit of Ayizan can take a long time to discover that they are possessed.

Ayizan is indeed a gentle soul, but some actions displease her and invoke her wrath. She hates adults that end up using young children, the poor, the weak and even abused wives. She punishes their actions.

We know that in Vodou culture, Ayizan is the wife to Loko, but to offer them respect and call on them in ceremonies is one of the more elaborate rituals in Vodou. This is because they are from the oldest lineage of spirits, and calling them jointly can be an intricate process. Also, because they are sticklers when it comes to Vodou tradition, the ceremonies and offerings need to be adhered to strictly as Vodou doctrine dictates.

Ayizan is considered more than just the first mambo, but also the guardian for all of the Vodou traditions in Haiti that originate from Africa. Because she is the spirit of the very first Vodou Priestess, you should call upon her using the name Mambo Ayizan. Remember that as a spirit of initiation and an ancient spirit, you want to make sure that you honor Ayizan first with an offering.

If you are trying to make offerings for minor issues, do not call upon Ayizan because she will not be bothered by you. She has more important processes that she handles as the spirit to the first Vodou priestess. The other duty of Ayizan is that as Queen of the Marketplace, she oversees the women who work in marketplaces and she manages their successes as well. She will offer protection to her believers against any envy and malice that others may want to bring upon them. Because she hates unjust acts against the poor, wives, weak, and children, she will take her wrath out on those who perpetrate the acts. Be very wary if you are the perpetrator and you seek to reach out to Ayizan, for she may take an even unkinder approach to you.

As the oldest and first Vodou priestess, she is a cesspool for information about the spirit world. She can be called upon to answer questions about the spirit world, but it is up to her choosing if she answers the call or not. Among Ayizan's amazing abilities, she can purify areas to make them sacred again.

In the religious images, Saint Anne is the picture that represents Ayizan. She is aligned with the color white and favors metals made from silver. When giving her offerings, you will offer her white flowers or spring water. Yams, bananas, and palm hearts can also work as well as the dirt that is gathered from outdoor markets. Ayizan is such an old spirit, so at times she is said to be paired with Legba. At the same time, the majority of Vodou stories have her as the mate of Papa Loko since she is a spirit of initiation ceremonies.

Papa Loko is the spirit of the first Vodou priest. A Vodou priest can also be called "Houngan." Like Ayizan, he is considered an old primal Lwa spirit, but he is also a magician and healer in Vodou history. Because of his status as the first Vodou priest, he is also considered a specialist about rituals and a top authority on the history and arts of the Vodou religion. Papa Loko guards the sanctuaries, rituals, and secrets of the Lwa family.

When he is traced back to his roots in Africa, Papa Loko was considered an ancestor of royal lineage. Yet, once he was incorporated into the religion that grew among the slaves in Haiti, his spirit took on a more profound association with religion and steered away from royalty.

Despite the similarity to the word "loco," Papa Loko's name has nothing to do with mental instability or craziness. In fact, it is an ancient name that's rooted in African origins. As you treat Ayizan with respect, so must Papa Loko be treated the same way.

This spirit has offered guidance and help to those who want to have a formal initiation into the Vodou religion, and he can be invoked for those who are seriously pursuing it. Likewise, he does not waste time or answer calls for those who are not serious about joining the realm of Vodou and being connected to all the branches of Vodou. The exciting thing about Papa Loko is that he always travels, accompanied by Papa Legba.

Papa Loko sympathizes and looks after males more than he does with his female counterpart. When trying to perform an offering, he is best served white rice or any white foods, herbs that pertain to healing, or any act that aligns with the reforestation of Haiti.

Together Papa Loko and Ayizan are the first mambo and the first Houngan. To perform Papa Loko and Ayizan's initiation ceremonies and rituals, their spirits are needed to guide the ritual. Their energies work together for their people, and as healers, they do the same. Papa Loko's healing technique lay with helping the body recuperate, while Ayizan's healing abilities work on healing the spirit.

Like Ayizan, Papa Loko is aligned with the color white, and that is why he prefers offerings in the color white. While Papa Loko might appreciate white rum, do not offer alcohol to Ayizan as she will not take it. She prefers waters and teas made from herbs. They work together in the spirit world to help in Vodou ceremonies.

Damballah

Damballah was a magnificent snake who lay underneath the Earth's surface. He was said to be the force that protected the Earth from falling into a watery death. He was the Earth's cushion in his first years. In fact, the story goes that Damballah was the very first deity of Earth. Even though he cushioned the Earth, he had to move and when he did the entire surface of the Earth changed.

As Damballah moved, mountains began to rise on the Earth's surface. That was not all that happened. As he moved around, valleys were formed; stars flew up into the sky, waters poured over the Earth and created rivers, streams, and oceans.

With all the changes that came around, the skies began to fill with water that would become rain. Amid the sun and the rain, a rainbow seemed to appear in brilliant colors in the sky. The rainbow, this being said, was actually Aïdo-Hwedo in disguise. She became Damballah's first love and in Vodou culture, and even today, they are still in love with one another. Their love was so overwhelming in their early days that it permeated the entire world and manifested in the very first human beings being formed.

Damballah is also known as the "snake Lwa of life." Damballah is associated with the beginning of life, but also wisdom and wealth. It is important to note that in Vodou, Damballah is very loved and foremost in the Lwa family.

Damballah's powers include overlooking the moisture and rain on the Earth as well as giving out wealth and good health. He is also stated to be capable of bestowing fertility on those that give him offerings in search of ability to conceive. Damballah and his partner uphold and maintain the balance of forces on Earth and help sustain the balance in life.

Don't bother Damballah with silly little issues because he will not partake in any pointless problems. Damballah is known to be wise and generous as he is such an ancient deity. Although he is the oldest deity and the beginning of life in Vodou, he still holds a great interest in humans and is always ready to help them out and overlook their marriages and relationships.

With how ancient Damballah is, he is not the world's best communicator through words. Sometimes he appears through our dreams, and you need to pay close attention to the signs to understand what he is telling you. Since Damballah was here from the beginning, this means that he was here before human speech and communication became part of human social behavior. When in your dreams or when communicating with him, you will hear sounds like hissing or even whistling, but he does not speak human languages that you are accustomed to speaking in.

If you are offering up to Damballah, keep in mind that he does like his surroundings to be clean, and he hates strong smells or smells that are offensive to the nose. He especially despises the smell of smoke from tobacco products. Usually, when offering up to Damballah, you will have an altar set up for him, so make sure to keep this altar clear and free of any strong odors or smoke debris. Flower odors that are light and not heavy are his preferred smell, and even if you just get water that is infused with a floral bouquet and keep it around his altar, that could help.

His form is that of a snake, and so his partner's appearance is a snake as well. Damballah's body is so humongous that like a snake, it forms seven thousand coils. Like the other deities we have covered, he also aligns with the color white. The best day to serve Damballah is Thursday. On your altar, when offering up to Damballah, the most traditional method is to create a hill of white flour on a clean white plate. It is critical that the plate is pristine in its white color. Then you will place a raw egg that has a white shell in the middle of the flour hill. Place this on your altar in service. Damballah also likes other white objects for his offerings, so white candles and white foods will also work.

Agwe and La Sirene

Agwe has many names, but the most common name he is called by is Met Agwe Tawoyo. He is known as the Great Admiral and the Sovereign King of the Sea. His kingdom is shared with La Sirene Diamant—she is a beautiful deity who many people say is Agwe's partner. Be that as it may, there is a debate on this topic with some Vodou followers believing that La Sirene is his daughter. Agwe and La Sirene are known as the royalty of the sea and in Vodou history are called the "Divine Royal Couple." They are manifested by the sea and are held to the waters of the ocean. Agwe, however, is more than the king of the waters and sea. It is believed that he is an admiral, even though his place is in the sea and not on Earth. Like Damballah, Agwe is an old spirit and one of the first. It is believed that as Damballah held the Earth together in his coils, Agwe existed in the waters that covered the Earth. He is a primal Lwa and among the first branches in the Lwa family tree.

In his position as admiral, Agwe is considered the admiral of the seas. Agwe has adapted throughout history to the human race and has changed the ways that he moves through the sea. In history, Agwe would travel through the water in a chariot made from the shell of pearls and drawn by dolphins. But now, as times have changed, he is seen in his boat that travels along the waters. The boat is always noticeable because his warriors and men surround the ship and every spirit on board the vessel obeys Agwe's command. On his boat and in the sea, Agwe's word is law.

Agwe like to be close to the people who earn their livelihood by and from the sea. Anything that happens on the sea and waters is because Agwe either commanded it or allowed it. Any altar that is set up for Agwe needs to reflect symbols of the sea and ships. They should contain shells and sand from the shores as well as pieces from ships (anchors, ship, and wheels). Agwe is also represented by wealth, and his altar can have gold coins or treasure chests by it.

When people need wealth from the world, they can call upon Agwe to help. He can help in this capacity because his waters are filled with lost treasures that are at his discretion to bestow upon those who are in need and who ask. Remember, if you do not serve him well, he is not likely to help you in your pursuit.

Agwe can also make himself known through possession, but he needs a chair to do so and a staff that he uses when he moves in the peristyle. He will greet everyone who is in attendance when he comes into possession, and when asked for advice, he is always quick to give it. Because Agwe comes from the water, he is considered to have foresight into the future. So, whenever he gives advice, it should always be listened to and followed because his advice stems from the visions that his foresight gives him.

Agwe, like many of the other spirits, is known by many names and occupies many different spaces in this realm. In Vodou, you will learn the phrase "Lwa se mister." This means that the Lwa are mysterious. So, remember that the Lwa has many mysteries that will never be revealed to us in this human capacity. Agwe is not only considered the master of the sea but also of the shore. From this, he is capable of creating earthquakes and has also been called the master of earthquakes and named the "Earth Shaker."

When offerings go up, it is customary to serve both Agwe and La Sirene. The best offerings that work are those that incorporate white wines or champagnes, mirrors, combs, and fruits that contain lots of water in them. Agwe likes to be served with songs and many prayers as well. Make sure, though, that the songs you are singing are being sung through sincerity and with love. Agwe does not like halfhearted attempts to serve him. If Agwe accepts what you have offered him, then you will see it sink out of your sight.

Agwe takes the form of an old man with a long white beard. His eyes are green, and despite his age, he is considered very handsome. He carries himself as a strict gentleman who commands respect and dignity from those around him. Agwe does possess the traits of kindness and patience, but still, with his rigid nature; he is also stern and does not tolerate disrespect. The ocean is the perfect embodiment for Agwe for it can be gentle and calm one moment, but brutal and unforgiving the next.

Agwe's origin also begins in Africa where he journeyed to Saint Dominique (now Haiti) during the slave trade. Agwe carried many souls home during this time, as many of the slaves that were moved to Haiti did not survive the boat trips. From this, he took on the job of carrying each person after their deaths.

La Sirene is called the Queen of the Sea and Song. She is also known as the beauty of the waves. You might find similarities in her name to the old myths that talk about sirens that lure men in the waters to murky deaths. Those stories stem from the one—La Sirene. She appears as a gorgeous woman on top of rocky outcrops in the sea. She will brush her long beautiful hair as she sits on the rock and views her reflection in the mirror that she carries. As the comb slides through her locks of beautiful hair, she sings an intoxicating song that draws the men to come toward her. La Sirene is known as a sexy temptress who lives amongst the depths of the sea but comes out to intoxicate the men around her.

Because of her intoxicating sound, she is considered the patron of music. The tone of her voice is known throughout the sea, and the men who answer her call become her lovers. La Sirene is more than just a beautiful face and voice. She is Agwe's counterpart, and as such, she also holds the wisdom and knowledge of the sea. Her clear-sightedness is spun into her songs, and she then sings these songs to her children so that they can also gain her wisdom.

Mambo Ayizan is the mother of the initiates, but Mambo La Sirene is the priestess spirit who will sing to the starts as they go below the sea and are about to be reborn. She sings to the initiates of her wisdom and the secrets that are held in the ocean. From her songs, the new initiates (which emerge as Houngan or mambo), will emerge from the waters with all the knowledge and tools necessary to carry out their duties.

La Sirene's beauty escapes the explanation of words, but she is more than a pretty face. Her power rivals that of the other deities, and as such, she is one of the most powerful of all Lwa. The Houngan and Mambo that are wise refuse to dip their heads underneath the sea waters for they are aware that La Sirene can whisk them away to her underwater realm. When this happens, it is believed that La Sirene takes them to her kingdom, so she can teach them the ways and magic of Vodou. She holds them for seven years before she allows them to return to the earth. When the Houngan or mambo reappears after seven years, they will have pale skin and white hair, but their skills will far surpass that of those who have not had La Sirene's teachings.

Like all queens, La Sirene does not travel the waters on her own. Agwe will always accompany her as she swims through waters, and so too will her mistresses: La Blanc, Zil, Ceverine, La Don, and Dereyale. It is important to note that La Sirene is an old spirit as well, and she too can come into possession. Regardless, she will not speak when she comes into possession, but she must be kept wet. If she becomes dry, she will begin to cry out in agony from not being near the water. La Sirene does not have legs, but rather a tail, so when she comes into possession; she will either be carried around the peristyle or will drag herself around as she sings the sounds of instruments.

When offering to La Sirene, you cannot provide to La Sirene without offering to Met Agwe as well. You will add the same things that I mentioned above for Agwe's basket, such as champagnes and sweet cakes. It is a crucial point that you never give them anything that came from the sea. This means that their offering should never contain fish, lobster, crab, or even seaweed. They are forbidden to offer to them as it is considered to already belong to Agwe and La Sirene. They love gifts and sweets that come from the land rather than the sea. So, if you want to offer up meat, you can try duck or lamb.

Ezili Freda

Mambo Ezili Freda is a powerful and beautiful member of the Lwa. Her entire name is Metres Mambo Ezili Freda Daome, but she is more commonly called Mambo Ezili Freda. Her full name pays reverence to her beauty.

Ezili Freda is the spirit that is the master of all romantic love, luxury, refinement, luck, and more. She is a stickler for everything being spick and span and does not like dirt around her or those that serve her. She is called more of a mistress because Ezili Freda acts like a mistress rather than a wife. Ezili is the wife of three men, meaning she has three husbands. They are Ogoun Feray, Damballah, and Met Agwe. On her hand, you will see she bears three golden rings, one meant for each of her husbands.

Ezili Freda is the ruler of all matters that concern the heart, so it makes sense that the ritual drawing for her is of a beautifully detailed heart. When in service, she can bestow romantic love to the seeker and even bless them with an abundance of riches that come with love. She is represented as a woman whose hair is long against her body and blonde in color.

Ezili is more than just a connoisseur of the heart. She is also known as a great magician and controller of magic. Her domains include that of material wealth and success, so she often can bless those who serve her with material possessions.

Since Ezili acts more like a mistress, she tends to dislike other women. When she comes into possession, she will avoid touching other women, and instead only saluting them or allowing them to press her pinky finger lightly in a refined manner. Ezili can be very, and it is not uncommon that she is the root of problems for men and women in relationships. She is often jealous when she considers other women as beautiful or when they have a man that Ezili wants; she will cause havoc in the lives of the women who fall under her scrutiny.

Despite her dislike of women, Ezili still has many children that are female as well as those that serve her. She is kind and generous to them. Her actions with men, however, are in stark contrast to her interaction with women. She will hug and kiss on men, marrying other men often when she can.

Ezili comes across as a very sweet Lwa, with a delightful personality. But as mentioned, Ezili has another side to her, and this can be dangerous as she is a very powerful mambo. Her magick is considered extremely powerful and potent, and when she is working with magick, it always gets done quickly with results. But her methods are complicated, and all of her services must follow her exact needs precisely. If they fail, then she will not help with your task.

Ezili aligns herself with white and pink colors because she is a flamboyant Lwa. She loves that which is refined, and her desire for perfection is what makes her so difficult to serve at times. When her needs are failed, she will cry in despair. Thursday is considered her dedicated day, so that is the best day to serve Mambo Ezili Freda.

Filomez and Klemezin

It is not uncommon for saints to become spirits of the Lwa. Such is the story of Filomez. She is a relatively new Lwa in that she did not become part of the family until Haiti was a free nation. Before becoming Filomez, she was Saint Philomena.

Saint Philomena was new in the Catholic family, but she was dropped almost as quickly as she was recognized. It was in 1802 in Italy when her relics were found. A thirteen-year-old girl was found in Saint Priscilla's catacombs. The body had a vial with dried blood on it. It wasn't until 1837 when the visions of a nun revealed her to be a martyr, was Saint Philomena canonized. Nonetheless, this did not last long, and she was removed from her position after Vatican II. At this point, in the regions of the Caribbean, worshipping Saint Philomena had already become second nature. And so, she was honored in Vodou. Her name took on the form of Filomez in Haiti. Her depiction in statues was that of a young girl or woman who would wear pink and have a palm frond or even an anchor near her.

Filomez has many different places in the realm of Vodou, with some placing her over prosperity as being the daughter of a merchant. At any rate, most of those who practice Vodou align her with Erzulie Freda and consider her a young sister to Erzulie.

When offering to Filomez, she prefers flowers that are pastel colored. She is popular in the Lwa family because she has a history in which she works miracles for those around her.

The next member of the Lwa has a fascinating story too. It was in 1212 when a young woman who belonged in the class of nobles ran away from her parent's home. Her name was Clare, and she lived in an Italian town called Assisi. She left her parents to follow a man, the same man who would later be called Saint Francis. Eventually, through her life and their denial of all natural objects, Clare became Saint Clare. She was also the founder of the Order of Poor Clares.

In 1253 Clare died; in spite of this, her memory far surpassed her death, and the legend of her life spread through the masses. The Order of Poor Clares was at first a place for women of nobility to gather. Subsequently, it soon became a place for wealthy families to send daughters that they deemed disgraceful or unfit for marriage. It became a small convent on the island of Saint Domingue shortly after the French had settled down to colonize it.

Through her grace in the Catholic Church, she entered into the Vodou realm as Lwa Klemezin. Contrary to her elderly and holy depiction in the Catholic Church, in Vodou, she is depicted as a spry young girl. Often times, when Klemezin takes possession, the one possessed will skip around the peristyle and jump like a child.

When serving her, she loves sweet cakes that have white icing. Light blue will also do for her. Flowers are her favorite items, and she loves them to be white or blue. When her servants need clarity and a clear head, they often call on Lwa Klemezin to help them and give them visions of the future. For psychic readings, she is always kept close to the reader. Klemezin is said to have a very energetic personality, but she is without fail, kind and loves to help those who give offerings to her.

Zaka

Zaka is also known as Papa Azaka. He is the Lwa that rules over all of the bonds that exist between Earth and the people who cultivate the Earth. He is also often referred to as a cousin in the Lwa family tree. Zaka is usually a trickster, but despite this, he is a generous spirit. Zaka works hard for his family and tends always to have a pleasant disposition about him. He does want to be served well with food, or he views that as slight disrespect. While Zaka is kind and generous, when he feels disrespected, he will turn nasty and become mean. Zaka is a mere peasant in the Lwa world, and he is suspicious of those who he thinks might want to rob him.

Most Lwa in the Rada rite hail from Africa, but Zaka's beginnings are actually said to have started in Haiti. As such, Zaka oversees all alliances that occur between the Haitians that are indigenous to Haiti and the Africans who were brought over in the slave trade.

Despite being a peasant, Zaka is still considered sacred. He might have some rough mannerisms, but he is still a powerful Lwa. He often appears in ragged clothes and acts like a poor beggar. This is often to judge how you will treat him and whether you will be respectful or be filled with disdain. When you treat him nicely, the same as you would the rich, and then you curry favor in his eyes.

When Zaka comes across people who are exploiting the poor to benefit themselves, he will see it fit to punish them. This is why he is a great ally and champion to the poor and oppressed. As long as you have respect for Zaka, in his small state, he will help you when you need it. Do not let your guard down, whatsoever, because as a suspicious spirit, he will continually test you. Sometimes these tests are with your requests. He might reject you just to see how you will respond to him. He does not want you to be fake with him but rather honest and upfront. When you displease him, he will give you symptoms of illness.

Since Zaka is the overseer of agriculture, he knows all of the secrets of the soil. He will often appear in dreams to help those who need instructions with carrying out herbal remedies and solutions. Zaka obviously has his preferences for the types of people who he prefers to interact with. To him, if you are a hard worker and earn your money through sweat and tears, you are a worthy person in Zaka's eyes. Zaka does like women, and he never wastes a chance to be a flirt with them. He will even help out women in need as long as they are respectful to him.

He is easily recognizable because he likes to wear traditional Haitian clothes. He is generally seen in blue jeans and a red scarf. He will don a straw hat and carry a bag over his shoulder. Sometimes he also walks around with a limp. When he is testing you, he will not be charming, but he will act aggressive and continue to bug you for food or money.

There are several women that Zaka is said to possibly be married to like Lwa Clairmeille or even his female partner Couzenne. Couzenne runs a market stand in the market area.

Zaka is associated with the colors blue and red, and the best day to serve him is on Thursdays.

You can create your altar to Zaka, but you can also just simply offer him a sack that is filled with things he likes, such as rum, brown sugar, and tobacco. Zaka does not really like perishable food to be offered to him in a serving. You should tie the bag with a red scarf and hang it up. Do not open the offering up unless you are adding more into the sack. As you are preparing Zaka's offerings, you should also talk to him so that he can feel comfortable enough to accept it.

When you offer to Zaka, do not be stingy. Be generous and offer him a large quantity because he is always hungry. Zaka will take perishable food in specific offerings, and when you do, it should be corn, rice, and bread. Because he is a laborer, he likes to eat a lot of food, so be prepared.

Do not taste his food when you are offering it to him. Zaka likes to taste and eat his food on his own. Sometimes you find that Zaka is asking you for something that you did not offer to him. If he begs you for it, simply give it to him. This can be like a little extra tidbit that you are offering to him.

Zaka also appreciates being given money. This is because he is scared about having no money for anything. When you are giving him cash offerings, place them in an envelope or even a money bag that you have created for him and put it either on his altar or underneath his statue. Once you do this, this cash is no longer yours to use and is gone. Do not try to take it or use it at a later date. If you need it, always ask him for permission before you take it.

Ogou

Ogou is an intriguing spirit because he is considered initially to come from the Nago people who were forced to slavery in Haiti. There are a lot of Ogou spirits in the Lwa world, but they are served the same way in the Rada rites. The interesting thing about Ogou spirits is that they can be personalized to a family, and a family can be of service to a specific Ogou.

Ogou is also capable of possession but will only possess the family that serves him. The most widely served Ogou is Ogou Feray, and he also frequently visits his family. Ogou Feray is considered Ezili Freda's partner and husband in Vodou culture.

Ogou Feray is considered the Lwa of war, and he oversees all battles that occur. He has the power to create and to destroy as he sees fit. When Ogou Feray possesses a person, he begins to yell. That is how he interacts with those around him. Because he oversees war and battle, he is usually considered a military general.

Ogou can expertly wield the machete, and it is his preferred weapon of choice. Ogou Feray is not all about war, he also shows his love for women. He will propose to them often while he is in possession. It is apparent that Ogou Feray represents masculinity as well, and he does not abide by frailty.

His association in the realm of the Lwa is fire. For the most part, they will build a fire during ceremonies that are meant to invoke the spirit of Ogou Feray.

The Petro Lwa

The Petro Lwa are amongst the most powerful and famous of the Lwa in the Vodou world. In fact, the Petro Lwa are called "spirits of revolution" as they were the spirits that were invoked during the uprisings in 1804 when Haiti was trying to win their independence. The Petro Lwa are spirits that came from Haitian soil.

Most of the Petro Lwa are spirits that originated from the Taino people who are the native people of Haiti. The Taino were the people who fought against the slave traders to earn their freedom. They wanted to make sure that Haiti won the title of the first black republic in the new world. There are many Petro spirits like Boukman, Mambo Fatima, Queen of Petro, and Erzulie Dantor who fought for Haitians to have their home again. Their blood was spilled so that their families could have a future.

The Petro Lwa are served all throughout Haiti, and they

have some of the most ancient rituals to follow in service to the Lwa. The Kanzo cycle is essential in the Petro rite, and we will get more in-depth with that soon in this chapter. The other ceremonies that you want to keep in mind are Bat Ge and Mere Paket as they are essential to the Petro initiations. These ceremonies prove the strength and power of their initiatives.

It is easy to tell when a Petro Lwa takes possession. They are demanding spirits, and as they come from the ancestors who fought the war for Haiti, they require a lot from their families. When they are displeased with you, they are quick to act out their displeasure, so when dealing with Petro Lwa, you want to make sure that you obey what they want and need the first time you are serving them. These spirits are usually served in blue and red as those are the colors of Haiti's flag.

Kalfou

Commonly known as "Master of the Crossroads," Met Kalfou is amongst the most pertinent Lwa in the Petro family. His name, Kalfou, is derived from the French word "Carrefour." The word literally means crossroads. You need to understand that his name means what he manifests as. Kalfou is the point of the crossroads, which is why he is such an important Lwa. Wherever roads cross and intersect, Kalfou is there. That is his manifestation.

Kalfou is fundamental to Vodou history as well as Vodou magic. To understand how strong Kalfou is, you first need to know how he is served. In Haitian secret societies, red and black represented the Petro Lwa. These same colors are used to benefit Kalfou in the Petro rite. Kalfou is considered a hot spirit, which means that he will only eat blood from the sacrifices made to him. He does often accept other foods in offerings such as apples that are blood red and cakes. These offerings are used to calm Kalfou down after he has been unusually hot. Kalfou very much so prefers the colors red and black and foods that coincide with those colors in the offering will bring Kalfou a lot of pleasure.

Offerings to Kalfou can be confusing because he likes them to be served distinctly, but it is essential that we serve him in the right way. Remember that he is a Petro Lwa. Therefore, he is enormous in his rituals being completed correctly. He likes to be offered things by a multiple of four. So, for example, if you provide Kalfou apples, you must make sure that they are four, eight, or even twelve apples. Do not give him an offering that is less than four or not a multiple of four. He hates uneven numbers.

Kalfou likes a particular drink called Kiman in his offerings. This drink is a Haitian Vodou drink made from white rum and white barbancourt with spices like cinnamon and star anise. Some houses have their own particular way of preparing Kiman, but as long as it is a hot and fierce drink, then Kalfou should readily accept it. It works particularly well if you want Kalfou to take possession.

Kalfou has a lot of rituals and ceremonies that are performed in honor of him and at the crossroads. Kalfou is considered a gad spirit, which means that he can help protect people from harm, but the ceremony needs to be performed to invoke his protection. Once Met Kalfou is protecting you, every single aspect of your life will be enshrined in protection.

Because of his fierceness and his tenacity, Kalfou is often mistaken as the devil or a demon of the devil. Some people also believe that Kalfou is a manifestation of evil, but this is an incorrect assumption about him. The reason he is sought to be evil is that he deals with the realm of magick as well, and he is well versed in magical works.

Kalfou's essence is the beginning of all magic. No magic happens that does not flow through Kalfou. Because he is the crossroads, he is the place where all things pass through. Simply, the magic could be used for good or bad, that is not up to Kalfou to decide. He is merely the manifestation that magic takes up.

When you think of Kalfou's association with magic, picture

him more as a conduit through which the magic travels rather than controlling it—because he has no control over the magic. He cannot judge what kind of magic is manifesting in his crossroads, and he must do his job, which is merely to help the magic pass through.

Despite being the crossroads for magic, Kalfou is also a great sorcerer on his own. He can work with powerful magic, but he does not use this power to manifest black magic; he upholds himself to high moral standards. Unfortunately, he cannot hold up all those who channel their magic to the same standard that he lives by. Kalfou accepts that humans have their own free will and can do as they please with their attained abilities.

Sometimes people will draw comparisons between Papa Legba from the Rada rite and Kalfou. But they are not the same Lwa and therefore should not be confused with one another. You see, unlike Legba, Kalfou is not a gatekeeper. He is only the manifestation of the point where the journey begins to split, and choices emerge.

Kalfou's crossroads are part of what is called the Vodou regelmen. During a Vodou ceremony, Gran Chemin is first invoked. This is the road that you will first walk along. Then, as you approach the door to Ginen, Legba is the one who unlocks this door. You will journey past the Marassa. They ensure that Ginen is being manifested in the rites. Finally, you will come to Met Kalfou where you will find the crossroads. As you reach the crossroads in a ceremony, it is up to you to make the choice of where you want to go.

Met Kalfou is a great spirit to invoke when you do it well. He is also the spirit of luck. When he is in possession, he will greet everyone present with the blessing "bon chans." This blessing means good luck. There are many different reasons to want to call Kalfou into possession, and depending on which goal you give to invoke him; he might act differently each time he comes into possession. Sometimes when he comes into possession, Kalfou will roll on the ground and do somersaults and jumps.

He is direct when he is speaking or interacting with a person, and he does not have the patience for those who are foolish. Remember that you want Kalfou on your side because he is a reliable and powerful Lwa.

Kalfou does give great advice and consultations, so when in doubt, he is an excellent Lwa to call upon to consult. The reason he is so good at this is that he loves to talk with people, despite his direct manner. When you ask him for help, he will eagerly help you so long as you have done your due diligence by him in your service and offering. Because he is a manifestation of crossroads, Kalfou can see what the outcome of various situations you might find yourself in are. So, he can guide you and advise you on what your actions will do for you depending on what you choose to do when you find yourself at a crossroads. When he is asked nicely, and in a good mood, Kalfou might even propel you to make the choice that best suits your life—this will be the choice with the most luck for us.

Met Kalfou is the reason the other Petro Lwa can come into possession for he is the one that brings them into the peristyle. Without Kalfou, they could not do this. This is another case why he is so prominent in the Lwa family because we would be unable to interact with our Lwa family without him.

Ezili Danto

Ezili Danto is a very popular Petro Lwa. She is a strict lady that can be tough to manage, but she is also a wild spirit. Ezili Danto is a mother spirit as well. Therefore, she manifests herself as the perfect mother that every person wishes to have. While she is a mother spirit and will watch over her family and protect them, she will also discipline those she watches over as she sees fit. Ezili particularly detests it when young children act out and misbehave. She is, after all, passionately loyal to her family and will often go out of her way to help them even if they have not sacrificed enough.

Ezili is often aligned with Madonnas in other religions, and she is also seen as Santa Barbara Africana; when serving her, that is the image to use for her. She has also been depicted as "Our lady of perpetual help."

She is a fervent defender of children and young ones. Just like a mother would protect her own offspring, Mambo Danto goes to extreme lengths to make sure that all of her children are kept safe and sound. If she is called upon, she will stop what she is doing to be at her child's side. Remember, as the Lwa are family spirits, all those in the family are considered her children. In any image of Danto, she is always depicted with a child.

Anais is Danto's most beloved child and the one who is most often captured in images and statues with her. Anais serves as her mother's translator and will interpret languages for her. When you are trying to speak to Danto, it is always good to serve and address Anais too so that you can pay the respect you need.

As I mentioned earlier, Danto can have a wild streak. Her personality can be aggressive, which makes her hard to control. Like Kalfou, she is thought to be a hot spirit. Danto remains independent and secure and is also considered a strong countrywoman.

Danto is considered a powerful Lwa who can sustain a great deal of damage in battle. Once it was said that she could take up to seven wounds and simply vomit blood but continued on with her task. When she possesses someone, she also likes to vomit blood, which becomes an easy way to tell when she has taken possession.

There are other Ezili's, and they can all get confused together as Vodou is an intricate religion. But Ezili Danto is entirely separate and not part of a group as the others are. She does have a lot of sister spirits that walk beside her and with her. On the other hand, that is common in the realm of the Lwa.

Ezili Danto and Ezili Freda have a longstanding rivalry that has plagued them for many centuries. Even though they are sisters, the two can barely stand to be in the company of one another. They argue over power, and each one is jealous over the other.

There is actually a story about these two sisters of Lwa. It begins as most stories do—with a male who got in between them. They were both seeing an Ogou Lwa, but they fought over who he loved more and since their fights about him, they could never reconcile with one another. As the two women battled over the Ogou Lwa, Danto brought a dagger into the fight, and she stuck it in Freda's heart. In Freda's image, to this day, there usually is a dagger that is made of gold that protrudes from her heart. As retribution, Freda grabbed the blade from her chest and slashed Danto's face open, permanently scarring her. The same scars are represented in the Santa Barbara Africana image, which depicts Danto.

Bossou

Bossou is also named Bossour Twa Kon and is considered to be the manifestation of power and enlightenment. Bossou's name derives from an old Dahomey kingdom. It is a place where King Agadja Dosou had a son named Bosou Achade. Bosou rose to be the ruler of the kingdom Whyda, so as his spirit moved to Haiti, he lost the King title and became simply Bossou.

Bossou's story is unusual in many ways because his name also refers to the fact that he was born with his mother's umbilical cord wrapped around his neck. His intrigue does not stop there, for he was known as a "tohosou," which means "touched by God." In Bossou's kingdom, whenever a child was born with any slight deformation, disadvantage or intrigue then they were thought to be an unusual child and that God had purposefully touched that child with his Holy Fire. These children were always considered to be more than human. Bossou had his own deformity, which is attached to the legend of his name—he had been born a hunchback. It looked like a bull was formed in his deformed shoulders, and this made people believe he had been touched by God.

Bossou is now a Lwa, and his spirit seeks to help those who cannot help themselves. Typically, when you are stuck in a place, and you see no way out, Bossou appears to help you bulldoze your way into a path that might free you. In this way, he is also considered a liberator as he offers freedom from things that might be restraining you in this life. He received the title liberator because he helped free his kingdom from those that sought to enslave them.

Bossou is aligned with the colors white, black, and red. He likes to be served in these colors. Bossou is also rumored to be the one who shoulders the world's burden, for he feels he has too. His image is that of a bull, which signifies solidarity and strength. The best time to make use of Bossou is in September. He is known to be particularly helpful to the sosyete (society), but he is also beneficial to the individual. If there is something you have wanted to complete but unable to push through, make sure that you invoke Bossou in September for he can help you with that.

Simbi

The Simbi are more than just one spirit. They hail from the Congo and are considered water spirits. These spirits are a large family, yet very diverse, and they are all powerful Lwa. Most Simbis that people interact with are male. Surprisingly, many people have still encountered female Simbis as well. The most significant Simbis are:

Lady Simbi, who is the matron to the Simbi family and is also called Gran Simba. She is Simbi's wife and a mother to their flock of forty children—all daughters. Gran Simba's spirit protects those who find themselves caught in the rapids and strong currents of the river. Also, if one falls into waters that will carry them to their death, Gran Simba will intervene.

Simbi Andezo's name comes from roots in the Kreyol version of the French word "Simbi en deux eaux." It stood for

Simbi in two waters, making Simbi Andezo as the spirit of fresh waters. These freshwaters can include any streams, rivers, and even smaller waterholes. But because his name is of two waters, he controls more than just fresh water. He also is the spirit of mangrove swamps where the water that is fresh and the salty water collide with one another.

The Saint that is used to depict Simbi Andezo is Saint Andrew. Whenever you serve Simbi, and you want to give him an offering, make sure that there are at least two different liquids that you serve him since he is Lord of more than just one water type. Usually, the offerings he enjoys will be water and whiskey. But, if you must, you can also give him the option of freshwater or saltwater.

He likes to be served in the colors of red and white or the colors green and red. Like his water cups, he must be served from two colors, or he will not listen to you, and your service will remain incomplete.

The herb-master for the Simbi is the Lwa Simbi Anpaka. Anpaka is considered the Lwa of all plants and medicinals, which include poison as well. His colors are white and green.

Simbi de l'Eau is the Kreyol for Simbi Dlo. He is considered the guardian of fresh water. Simbi Dlo can be a strong ally to those who need assistance defending an area where a freshwater source is a key to survival. His image is often linked to the archangel Raphael from Roman Catholicism. He likes to be served in red and blue, or he can be served in blue and green.

We cannot leave out the soldier-like representation, and for the Simbi this is represented in Simbi Ganga. He is known as a strong commander in chief. Simbi Ganaga is a warrior spirit, but he is also considered a guardian as he will protect you and that which needs protection. It is thought that he was previously a chieftain. He can be served in red alone or the colors blue and red.

Simbi La Flambeau is the Simbi of fire. While the Simbi spirits can be used by the Rada family, Simbi La Flambeau is considerably a spirit to just the Petro family of Vodou spirits. This Simbi is the Simbi of electrical fires. He controls all of the energy that is conducted through a person's body. Ordinarily, the Simbi will work with folk magic and sometimes earth magic, but La Flambeau is considered a master magician—particularly when it comes to ceremonies. When you serve Simbi La Flambeau, make sure to offer him things like rainwater that was caught from lightning storms only. You can also provide the skins of snakes and rum. He does like most beverages that are alcoholic in nature. If you are offering him food, make sure that it is spicy and add some hot sauces to it. All of his offerings must be tightly closed with red ribbons. He will be served in red as well as that is the color he associates with.

The great shaman and sorcerer of the Simbi spirits is Simbi Makaya. He is served by the Haitian secret societies. Interestingly enough, there are also Vodou traditions and rituals that are named after Makaya. Makaya earned his name as a revolutionary since historically he is considered to have led the revolution against the slave owners. He was the leader of the slaves in Haiti that had escaped. But they did not stay in hiding, and together with Makaya, they would charge into battle against their oppressors.

When you are giving up offerings to Makaya the simplest way to do so is to plant trees in his honor and offer this as his offering. He wants to see the forests in Haiti restored. You can serve him in black, red, or green.

Grand Bwa

Grand Bwa has many variations on his name, like many of the Lwa spirits do. Another common way of spelling his name is Gran Bois. Gran Bois is thought to be the father of the forest and is a healer who uses his knowledge of all plant secrets to help heal those in need. The power of the forest boosts his healing capabilities. Grand Bwa is considered an old and ancient Lwa, but with that, he is also a very authoritative spirit as well. His origins are a little murky, with some saying he is from Congolese origin and others saying that he was a Taino spirit from the people of Haiti.

He is thought to be the head of the Vodou's Congo as well as to the pantheons of the Petro rite. He is also a patron to the initiation of others into the Vodou religion. Grand Bwa is part of a trinity of magicians; he is the third amongst Baron Cimitiere and Maitre Carre-four.

Because of his connection to the forest and how ancient he is, often Grand Bwa is called the tree of life. He manifests as the tree of life that connects the realms of the living and the dead to one another. He is not just the ruler of the forests on Earth, but he also rules Ginen, which is the realm that our Vodou ancestors go to. There is no secret of life or death that Grand Bwa does not know about.

When he is depicted in images, he is shown as Saint Sebastian; the saint that was bound into a tree. As Grand Bwa manifests, he takes on the appearance of a man who is half a tree and half man. Like Damballah in the Rada rite, Grand Bwa is such a primordial spirit that he comes from a time of pre-speech, so he does not talk as other spirits do.

When you serve him, he is served with the colors green, brown, and red. The Mapou tree is considered especially sacred to the Grand Bwa as there were attempts to decimate the existence of the tree. This is because, in 1940, it was believed that this was an essential tree in the practice of Vodou and in an attempt to remove Vodou from their belief system, the church sought to destroy all Mapou trees.

Grand Bwa likes food offerings, such as cornmeal with honey, leaves, roots, and even cassava bread. He will also take tobacco, but the best way to serve him is to ensure the preservation of his forests.

Ibo

Gran Ibo is a powerful Lwa who gathers strength deep inside what is called the sacred swamp. This is where she makes her home. The Lwa Ibo is considered to be the mother of the

Ibo people. She taught them (and continues to teach those who come now) how to free themselves from the chains that were holding them down so that they may arise. Ibo wields powers of plants and herbs that possess healing capabilities. She also grows her own healing herb garden. While she does hail from Africa in her origins, it is believed that her real place was meant to be as part of the Haitian Vodou Lwa spirits.

Where the chains come into play in the Ibo's story comes through the history of the Ibo people. The Igbo people rebelled against invasion at a place called Dunbar Creek. As they were all chained up and being led into the waters to die, they called upon the Great Choir God to protect them from what was coming. They were all marched into the waters chained together where their spirits were released from suffering, and the water spirit brought them to their home and peace. This is why Gran Ibo works hard to free those of the chains that hold them down.

Djabs

Djab is a Creole word that essentially means devil as it comes from the French dialect. It is an extremely loose translation, but nonetheless, this is the name that Djabs have been branded with. Djabs are considered more of a dark area in the Vodou world rather than a real spirit. When dealing with Djabs, it is crucial to know a few things: firstly, there are many different Djabs spirits, and secondly, they do not all have good intentions.

A Djab in the realm of Vodou is considered to be a person's own personal spirit. These spirits decide to attach themselves to families, and they serve them—either with good will or maliciously. A Djab is another family spirit that passed down from each generation to the next and must be treated as a member of the family. Sometimes this can be trying when the Djab that is attached to you is malevolent because it will take work to make sure that the Djab stays out of trouble or chained to good behavior. The reason is that Djabs are considered to be spirits that usually are sent to bring misery and not a joy to those that they attach to.

It is hugely suggested that you go through an experienced person if you want to contact a personal Djab or see if you have one attached to you. The reason is that you do not want the dark spirited Djabs to gain footholds in your life and an experienced Houngan or mambo can help make sure they are correctly tamed. If, without question, you find that your Djab is amiable, then you should try and get to know them. They can be helpful entities.

The Gede Lwa

The third main branch of the Lwa family is the Gede Lwa. The Gede are very loving spirits in the Haitian Vodou realm. Their spirits embody those of the dead that have been forgotten or that have no one left to remember them. These spirits were reclaimed by the Baron and brought into his entourage to celebrate and dance.

The Gede Lwa are said to be the personification of all that is life and will be life. These are spirits of fertility, and they help ensure healthy deliveries for those that are expecting. The Gede, after all, are more than just fertility spirits. They embody the spirits as well as all that is intimate and sexual. They are the manifestation of the act where one conceives. There is raw sexuality that vibrates off of the Gede. While the Gede Lwa cannot partake in the act of sex themselves, the dance that they perform, which is known as the Banda, imitates the act of sex.

To the Gede, now that they have ascended to being Lwa, they are no longer bound by the limitations that they were as humans. There is nothing that is forbidden or impermissible to the Gede. They love to live, have fun, and laugh.

Not only are they experts at defining raw sexual energy, but they also love to tell dirty jokes. Their jokes can be very raunchy and are said to make even the roughest sailor blush. Whenever the Gede are around, it is said to be a joyous celebration full of feasting and eating and having fun.

While the Gede Lwa are free spirits who have abundant joy and love a good party, they are more than just merely jokers.

They are the spirits of death, and as such, they are also great healers. When someone is dying before their time, the Gede Lwa and help heal them, even if they are on the very verge of death. The Gede Lwa love to be around children, and they honor them as the future of the world and of humanity. If a sick child is brought to them, they will heal them as quickly as they can.

Even if the sickness is rooted in magic or because of a spiritual reason, the Gede Lwa spirits will be able to help remove the cause of the dangerous magic or even the evil spirit. Once they lift bad spirits from you, they will cast it back to the grave it belongs to.

Some of the best diviners come from the Gede Lwa, and they are wise beyond what they seem. They are always a great resource to turn to when one needs help or has questions that they need answers. The great thing about talking to the Gede is that you know they are incapable of lying as they are bound to the truth. Sometimes these results in brutal honesty, so one must be prepared to listen to what they have to say.

Because the Gede Lwa are comprised of spirits of the dead, there are so many Gede that it is almost impossible to count and explain who is who and how many there are.

The Ghede

The Ghede are also called mysteries and invisibles. When directly translated, the word Ghede means "the sacred dead." There is a celebration called the Festival of the Ancestors that usually is completed on the second day in November each year. This festival honors the Lord of the Dead and is called "Fete Ghede." The significance of this festival is that it is used as a way to repay the Ghede for all of the blessings that they have provided for you for the year. It is indispensable not to skip doing Fete Ghede because if you do, then the Ghede spirits will take their revenge on you.

The Fete Ghede celebration includes a spiritually led procession into the cemetery. All of the Houngans, Mambos, drummers, and singers will pray together at the cemetery. Usually, it is at the foot of a cross that rises from a tomb. This is to summon all of the Ghede spirits to the party or celebration.

As mentioned above, Ghede Lwa's most extraordinary power is that of their ability to heal, to predict or see the future and then to protect their family members.

Ghede Linto is the Lwa of miracles and can often be found performing miracles to save his people. Ghede Loraj's spirit often rescues people who are caught in dangerous storms. Ghede Doubye blesses those that he believes are fit to carry the gift of second sight or clairvoyance. Papa Ghede is the spirit of the first man who died and became a Lwa. As he is the first spirit to die, he is called the guider of souls. He likes to smoke cigars and can be seen eating apples quite often. Papa Ghede will sit at the crossroads waiting to take the new souls into the spiritual realm. Brav Ghede Nibo is known to be a fantastic healer for the Ghede Lwa.

Other famous Ghede, such as Baron Kriminel, Maman Brigitte, and Ghede Masaka all had a hand to the greatness and the diversity of the Ghede Lwa. The Baron is known as a murderer, where Brigitte is considered a mother that protects crosses and the gravestones of the dead. Then there is Ghede Masaka who is known as the gravedigger. He can be recognized easily because he always wears a white jacket, a white scarf on his head, and a black shirt.

The Bawon

The Baron is called many different names. He is known as Bawon, Bawon Lakwa (which means Baron of the Cross), and even as the Criminal Baron. When manifesting the Baron, the image of Saint Expedite is used.

The Baron is the Lwa spirit of the dead. It is said that the spirit of the very first mortal male to die was the Baron, while the spirit of the very first female mortal to die was Maman Brigitte.

He rules over all of the cemeteries where the dead are

buried, and he is the main Lwa of the Ghede rite. Even though there are a specific festival and day for the Ghede spirits and the Baron, it is essential to know that they are generally served throughout November and not just on one day.

He is associated with black, purple, and white colors. When symbols are needed to represent him, either a cross or a coffin may be used.

There is a distinct difference between Papa Legba and the Baron, and this difference must be noted for they are not the same Lwa. Papa Legba opens up the doors from the realm of the Lwa to the field of humanity. He says who can and who cannot pass through the doors to communicate with society.

The Baron is simply the first soul of the first dead mortal man. When you need legal help, it is also helpful to invoke the Baron as he is excellent at creating justice for those who need him.

Brigitte

Brigitte is also known as many names. Her most common name, however, is Mamam Brigitte. She is noted as the Queen of the Cemetery as well as the Queen of the Spiritual Realm. Brigitte's husband is Baron Samedi, and they are often seen together or sought out together for issues such as fertility and healing. Some people are scared of Baron Samedi, and this is where Maman Brigitte will take over to keep your fear in control. They are also used to help and guide children who fall terminally sick.

While she often works alongside her husband, she is no weakling, and she is not dependent on him. Brigitte has impressive powers of her own. Brigitte was first known as Brigid, a woman who was forced into Haiti by the Scottish and the Irish. But while in Haiti, Brigid evolved into a Lwa and she married the Baron Samedi. When songs are sung about Brigitte, they still pay honor to her country of Scotland where she first hailed from. Maman Brigitte has an active presence in places such as

New Orleans where she was carried there by Haitians who were seeking refuge.

For those who have sons and daughters serving in the military, they can invoke Maman Brigitte to look after and protect their children. She is also sometimes called upon to bless a family with financial prosperity when times are desperate.

Comparable to the Baron, Brigitte also serves justice, and she is an active judge in the Court of Spirits. If a judgment is required but has eluded you, you can invoke Maman Brigitte and seek her help and guidance.

Her image manifests as Mary Magdalene, and when she is needed to be represented, that is the image to use for Maman Brigitte. She materializes as a white woman in the realm of Vodou.

Maman Brigitte is to be served on Mondays, Wednesdays, and Saturdays. She is tended in black or shades of purple with violet being amongst her favorite color.

If you wanted to create an altar for Brigitte, you must do so in a cemetery. You would merely arrange rocks together in little pyramids that will act as an altar for Brigitte. You can alternatively also bring rocks back from the graveyard to your altar at home to create one in your private space.

When offering up in service to Brigitte, she likes black coffee, rum that has been infused with hot peppers, violets, purple irises, red wine, and purple eggplants. She will also accept black beans, cornmeal, and roasted corn.

The Ancestors

The Ancestors are incredibly crucial in Haitian culture and in Vodou. In fact, they are so important to honor that Haiti's own national anthem pays homage to the ancestors. It goes, "For the country, and for the ancestors, we walk united." That right, there is indicative of how seriously Haiti takes their ancestors.

Haiti's countryside is full of graveyards, and these graveyards are considered family graveyards. If you visited them, you would see tombs for the family members who died in as elaborate a fashion as each family can afford to do. There are elaborate tombs that are built above ground like smaller houses with stairs descended into the crypt underground. Some wealthy families have sitting rooms or living rooms in their tombs, and the graves are covered in pictures of those who have passed away. If you are visiting any family compound, then it is customary that you pay respect at the tomb of the ancestors so that they too may welcome you as a visitor.

It is not uncommon for families or even guests who are visiting to pay homage and make what is called an illumination by the tomb (you will learn more about lights and illuminations here shortly).

For families that live in the city and not in the country, they are forced to bury their dead in the city's cemetery. Nevertheless, this does not prevent them from creating detailed structures for their ancestors. You can even see particular tombs with padlocks on them so that they act as a deterrent for grave robbers in the city. Grave robbers go after the bones and other trinkets that are placed with the dead; the reason for this is because these bones of the ancestors are considered to possess magic. Their bones are even more coveted if the person that died was a Houngan or even a mambo.

The Baron is the head of the ancestors, and he guides them all as he is considered the master of the cemetery. He takes form in Baron Samedi, Baron Criminel, and other Baron's as well. Each version of him is depicted as masculine and dominant. His voice is said to be nasally, and he is always seen carrying a stick to walk with. This Lwa will often swear when he is speaking and is distinguishable because he dresses only in black or purple. Families will invoke Baron as a last ditch effort or a last resort to protect them against death. If the Baron will not dig a person's grave, then it is said that the person's time to die has not yet come.

The Baron and Maman Brigitte make up the heads of the ancestral Lwa of the Ghede.

The Other Lwa

You should be familiar, at this point in time, with the word "Lwa." The Lwa are the essence of Vodou and at the core for everything that Vodou is and what it accomplishes. Because Vodou uses the Lwa spirits does not mean that God is not an original concept—he is. Subsequently, God is considered a very distant and intangible being that is not available for humans to interact with.

Because Vodou is not seen as a separate religion to Roman Catholicism, it is not surprising that they share the same God, and both faiths view God in a similar light. The Vodou religion also believes that God is good and kind and that he loves humans. For all that, they see him as inaccessible since he has an entire world to take care of. Where Vodou takes a turn is that they believe that God placed some of his power in the spirits that are called Lwa.

The Lwa are the spirits that we have access to and that we can interact with. They are by their core definition a spiritual deity. The Lwa can take possession of a person, but it is important to note that this is not done in a demonic way. The Vodou priests and priestesses seek possession to happen, so they can communicate with the Lwa. At Kanzo (which we will elaborate on shortly), the possession of a Lwa is needed and wanted to say that the candidate is worthy of their initiation.

I think it is essential to draw the distinction between worship and servitude. The Lwa are not worshipped by Vodou practitioners, but noticeably they are served by them. The Lwa are provided with their favorite foods and colors, and their sacred days are watched and observed. Many Vodou ceremonies are performed in honor to them. All of these acts are in favor of serving the Lwa who do so much for each family. It is almost a direct exchange for services in this way. The Lwa are served, and in return, they will provide a service by protection, wisdom, or even material abundance. It is a relationship where both sides need one another, and without one side, the other will fail to exist.

To make serving the Lwa a lot easier, they are organized into family groups. Each Lwa has their own characteristics and personalities. They also only serve the family to which they are ancestors of. We have already gone over several of the Lwa groups like the Rada Lwa, the Petro Lwa, and the Gede Lwa. Remember those distinctive personalities? Most of the Rada Lwa are from African descent that traveled to Haiti. The Rada Lwa are also considered passive spirits who prefer to be defensive rather than take an aggressive stance.

The Ogou Lwa fits in the Rada Lwa liturgy. Despite that, they are their own family of spirits as well. These spirits descended from the Nago nation, and instead of being a specific family Lwa, they serve and mainly belong to their Nago nation. The Ogou Lwa hail from Nigeria and many spirits take on the name Ogou. These Lwa have an entirely separate way of performing rituals, songs, and even drum beats!

The Petro Lwa are a fundamental group of Lwa as well. They are more aggressive than their Rada Lwa counterparts, which causes them to act against enemies a lot faster than the Rada spirits would. In fact, while there are a lot of differences in personalities with these two Lwa family spirits, the most significant difference comes from their history and origins. The Petro spirits are from the Congo and the Kreyol versus the Rada who come from African descent. While there are a few Petro spirits that do come from Africa, the spirits are a mixture of many different nations and not just one land in particular.

The Gede Lwa are one of the last groups of the prominent Lwa families. These Lwa are a family with the Baron and Brigitte at the head of the family spirits. Baron and Brigitte oversee the rebirth of the Gede family members as Gede Lwa. There are so many Gede Lwa because they are continually adding more Lwa to the Gede family as more humans in the Gede family pass away.

Djabs are another type of spirit, while they are not directly a Lwa, sometimes a Lwa spirit can take on traits of a Djab and end up being named as one for their aggressive nature. Typically, Djabs are not Lwa. They tend to be more personal spirits that attach to a specific person. The Djabs do not follow any spiritual guidelines, but their focus is more on performing and increasing magical abilities. Djabs are dangerous spirits to work with, regardless, since they are aggressive and vindictive. When they feel slighted or do not feel appropriately served, they will punish you as they see fit.

THREE

Vodou in Haiti Today

Haiti is still embroiled in times of injustice and pain today. There have been epidemics that have riddled the population of Haiti, such as cholera. These epidemics claim tens of thousands of lives each year.

There are incredible injustices performed against those with disabilities and even women. They see violence every day, and many Haitians struggle to survive and provide their families with enough sustenance to be healthy. Even shelter can be a problem - particularly with how Haiti has been ravaged not only by crime and violence but also by natural disasters. But, despite all of that, Vodou still finds a way to persevere and uplift the people in Haiti. They express themselves in their beliefs through dancing, singing, and other forms of music. Vodou has now become a way to move past all of the pain and struggle that has plagued Haiti and continues to do so.

Peristyle

Vodou ceremonies are performed in what is called a peristyle. A peristyle is a Vodou temple. These temples are typically hidden or tucked away for privacy and so that the whole world does not interrupt their ceremonies and rituals. It can be hard to find peristyles unless someone who takes part in the Vodou ceremonies introduces you to them.

Luckily, Vodou priests are happy to educate the public and those unfamiliar with it about the real Vodou art that they practice. The Vodou that is not about violence as Hollywood would suggest, but rather peace, healing, and relief from pain. Make sure that if you interact with a priest or priestess that you show them the utmost respect. Favors can go a long way in displaying respect.

Many ceremonies are kept a secret, and that only occurs when no one is around to see. This is because the Vodou rituals are very intimate ceremonies between the families and the Lwa, and they are not for the amusement of other people. Even ceremonies that are performed in the open can be intimate and personal. There are sometimes ceremonies that do require animal sacrifices — these sacrifices are usually a chicken or similar bird. By sacrificing the animal, they believe that life is being released into the Lwa spirits and serves as a source of rejuvenation. Most Vodou ceremonies happen at night in the dark and can last into the early hours of the morning when the dawn starts to rise. It can be hard to stay up for newcomers, but once you revel in the celebration of the ceremony, the energy flowing through your body will keep you up.

FOUR

Haitian Vodou Ceremonies and Rites of Passage

Serving the Lwa

The Lwa are served in many variations of ways on their own sacred days. You must recognize their days by wearing the right color for the Lwa spirit that you are serving. Abstinence is also observed on a day when you are serving the Lwa. You usually will accompany this with songs and ceremonies. There are even some people who are married to a Lwa spirit, and these people have an obligation to their Lwa to observe their day.

In Vodou religion, Monday is not the first but the second day of the week. Monday is a sacred day for the ancestors, the Gede Lwa, and Legba. These are the Lwa that are traditionally served first before other Lwa are served. This is because they view Sunday as the first day of the week and the day that God should be served (since he comes first). Following God, you then serve your other Lwa in their own order of importance. Because Legba is the gatekeeper, he must be served before all the other Lwa otherwise it is fruitless to try and communicate with the other Lwa spirits for he will not let them.

A lot of Vodouisants (those who practice Vodou) perform devotionals each day to their Lwa. By doing devotionals, they were simply waking up their Lwa family spirit to work for them. Devotionals are personal and can take many different forms.

Make sure that your offerings and your altars are clean and fresh. If you have offerings such as water or liquids, make sure to replenish and refresh these offerings so that they do not go stale. Candles around the altar should be lit as they are needed, mainly if you are doing a devotional to your Lwa. Don't forget to talk to them. Your spirits want you to speak to them and make them feel comfortable as well.

Learning Vodou and how to serve takes time. It is a religion that is steeped in rituals and traditions. You need to give yourself time to learn and appreciate the customs so that you may adopt and adapt to them as your own. Vodouisants always face their problems head on, and they do not run away from them. Their service to the Lwa helps give them the support they need to take care of and conquer the issues that plague them.

Usually, Tuesdays are reserved for Petro spirits. In particular, Ezili Danto must be served on Tuesdays. The Ogou Lwa who come from the Nago Nation are served on Wednesdays. The Rada Lwa are served their offerings on Thursdays. When Friday comes around, the Gede Lwa are once again served. Saturdays are free days where all of the Lwa can be served. Remember that you only have to serve the Lwa which pertain to your family and which you want to build a relationship with.

Haitian Vodou Magic

The Lwa have a saying about Vodou magic. This saying is that anyone in the world can benefit from having the insight and healing of the Lwa spirits. This means anyone in the world. You do not have to be born and raised in Haiti to benefit from the Lwa spirits. You can attend ceremonies, eat, dance, and pay homage to the Lwa spirits that you want to encounter. It is simple to understand the ways that every single person is welcome to celebrate the Lwa spirits. The catch comes into play when we start talking about leading ceremonies, being possessed, and taking part in the proceedings.

These positions are generally harder to come by, and not everyone can do them. Vodou welcomes the world, but it is essential to realize that it is also not a religion that speaks to everyone. Everyone will not embrace and partake in the rituals of Vodou.

If you are on the outside and you want to know how to transition into the world of Vodou, then there is a lot to learn. It can be hard to distinguish if you wish to benefit just one day or whether you plan to benefit for the rest of your lifetime. Is Vodou going to be something that you embrace body and soul?

The first steps are always the hardest because you never quite know in which direction to step or where to take your faith. That is why there are resources like this book, so you can learn more about what to do when you are first entering the world of Vodou or even if you are merely curious about the process of it.

The first question you need to ask yourself before you embark on this journey is if Vodou is really what you are in search of. It makes all the difference if you understand what you are searching for or what your end goal is when you dip your toes into the pool of Vodou.

Most of the time, people are curious about understanding what folk magic is all about, and not the religion that is Haitian Vodou. But there is a distinct difference, and Vodou is not folk magic. It is its own religion with a system of beliefs and powerful family spirits that work together.

Vodou — like any other religion - does have its own hierarchy when it comes to the people on Earth who practices it. For example, the priesthood is one of the highest levels of authority you can attain in the religion of Vodou. When priests complete magic, they make use of the help of the Lwa spirits. Their magic is never accomplished on the priest's own abilities. Because their magical ability is strictly derived from the power, the Lwa spirits grant them. This ability to work with magic is not something that all that follows the Vodou religion can do.

So, this is why it is essential to clarify to yourself what you really want to learn about.

There is folk magic called "hoodoo" (very similar to Vodou and why it gets so often confused) that will be more suited to those who want to practice magic and learn about conjuring or root magic. If you are seeking, for example, a relationship with the spirits of the Lwa, then you might be interested in the Vodou religion.

The Lwa offer a community of family and connections to those who might be lacking or who need to feel more connected to their spiritual ancestors. It can be hard to know if the Lwa are calling to you and then even harder to understand how to answer that call. This is where it is crucial to remember that Vodou does not discriminate based on your background. It is for anyone. You do not have to be from Haiti to learn and adopt the Vodou religion. Ginen is a realm that can reach all over the entire world, and to this day touches countless lives around the globe. They can be calling to you right now even if you have never experienced the culture of Haiti and do not yet fully understand the religion of Vodou.

Typically, the Lwa will call out to you in your dreams, so they can learn more about Vodou. Sometimes Papa Legba might appear to you, trying to guide you into the way of the Lwa. The Ghede Lwa can also do this as they are a more universal Lwa than the other two rites.

I will suggest to you a word of caution here. If Vodou is the religion that you want to partake in, then you must be careful about misinformation. Always double and triple check sources and never try to serve the spirits on your own without the background knowledge. As you should well know by now, if you serve a spirit incorrectly, you might just incur their wrath. That is not how you want to start your relationship with them.

The best way forward for you is to find a Houngan or Mambo that you can reach out to and correspond with. Meeting in person is better, but with the power of the internet, it is possible to discover resources to communicate with a priest or priestess that way. They will help guide you and interpret the messages that the Lwa are sending to you through your dreams. As an inexperienced person in Vodou, your best ally is a person with the most experience. The Houngan or Mambo are there to help you as an uninitiated individual to start your relationship with the Lwa. They are there to teach you, to guide you, and to propel you into a relationship and world that exceeds what your mind can conjure up on its own. The Lwa gives them the information and the tools that they need so that they can be your best asset in the world of Vodou.

There is a reading that must be performed by a Houngan or Mambo called an escort consultation reading. This is where they can differentiate with spirits and Lwa are calling you and walking with you. It might also be an easy way to decipher the messages that the Lwa are trying to tell you. Sometimes the Lwa will call you to Vodou, but they will also determine how you must rise in the world of Vodou. You might need to learn all you need to be an initiate. If this is where you are called, then you become an initiate in the ranks of priesthood. Sometimes you will be called merely to be a Hounsi (a house member) to serve the Lwa. Hounsi can also be possessed by the Lwa at ceremonies, and they are assistants to the Houngan and mambo. There are much variability in what you might be called to do.

The Houngan or Mambo will be your first step to determining the direction that you go in. Maybe you are called to the priesthood, or perhaps you are called to start building a relationship with a particular Lwa. The job of the Houngan will be to guide you so that you have the best success and know how to serve your Lwa.

Be careful of the fraudsters who will trick you into believing that they are a true Houngan or mambo. When you are not there in person, it can be hard to decipher if a person is a true mambo or not. Make use of the internet and your ability to connect and research at the touch of a button. You will need to do your part of working to make sure that the person you choose to help and guide you is a real and genuine person and not a fraudster or a fake. This can be difficult to do, especially for someone new to Vodou.

The best way is to begin building your relationship with Legba. Do your research and learn all about him because as the gatekeeper, he can help show you when a person you are reaching out to is a real Houngan or a fake. Legba will help guide you into the road that is the right path for you.

Sometimes reaching out to your ancestors can be helpful, but without previous knowledge of how to do that, it can become tricky to try and rely on your ancestors for help. Just know that they have your best at heart and will often try to make sure that you are directed to the correct individual to assist you with your spiritual journey.

Sometimes it is the Ghede Lwa who will call you to Vodou; in this case, your ancestors definitely will be your best resource for help. The reason for this, if you recall, is that the Ghede spirits are spirits of the dead.

Patience is a virtue that you will practice during this time. Nothing will happen instantly or out of the blue. You need to start educating, researching, and practicing how to connect with the spirits and how to be open and receptive to their communication to you. The signs will be there leading you in the right way, but they will mean nothing if you are not listening and looking out for them. They can be subtle, so subtle that you are easy to miss out on them if you do not pay attention.

When you have connected with the right Houngan or mambo, and you have had them read your consultation to you, you will be presented with a roadmap of where your spiritual journey needs you to go. You might need to put in more time learning and more work into your journey into the religion of Vodou, but no matter what it is, the picture will now be clear to you. This is also when you are going to begin building a relationship with your Lwa. Your Houngan or mambo can guide you in this, or you could attend a fet to learn more.

What is a fet? Well, if you have not yet surmised it, a fet is merely a party that is held in celebration of one or more Lwa on their dedicated day. All those who follow Vodou religion and build relationships with particular Lwa will come together on these days and dance and sing as well as pray to their Lwa. Their prayers are calls to the Lwa so that the Lwa will go down and take part in the festivities.

This is also an opportunity for Lwa to take possession. A Lwa that takes possession usually is there to give out advice and guidance to the attendees that need it the most. When the Lwa do arise in possession, they often give guidance, advice, and healing to those who invoked their spirits. There are plenty of benefits to taking part in a fet once you know the Lwa you are serving. You can gain insight into what Vodou religion looks like and how the community can come together with one another. You will also understand how each member in the Vodou religion has their own place and part to play. Every skill is used as it best fits the community and to give glory to God and offer service to the Lwa. If you find yourself being drawn and your heart being called, then you might find that you belong in the Vodou religion.

Your road into Vodou is entirely dependent on God and the Lwa. You must seek out your path to know where your journey will take you and what your place is going to be in the world of the Lwa spirits. How far the path unfolds is up to the Lwa as well as to God. Still, how seriously you decide to walk forward, it is up to you. If you do partake in the Vodou religion, then you can be comforted by the fact that you will never again be alone. In fact, you will be surrounded not only by God and the ancestors but by the Lwa who will protect you.

The Family, Initiation, and Practice of Vodou

It is a big deal to be initiated into a particular house or family once you join the Vodou religion. When you are initiated, you are served with many blessings, but one of the biggest blessings is that your relationship with the Lwa will become a more intimate one. You will also gain a better understanding of Vodou and how Vodou is a family, and you are connected to all those in your family. When you are initiated, a sacrifice from you is required. You will now be giving a part of yourself and your life to Vodou, the Lwa, and the house that you serve. This, however, is a sacrifice that you receive back tenfold because it will be to the betterment of yourself as a whole.

You can seek out to be initiated on your own, or you will find that a Lwa is calling you to initiate. There is a specific ceremony you need to go through; the lave tet (which we will go into detail about soon). You might find that you are called into priesthood, but you must always follow the steps before you can be initiated no matter how you are selected to serve.

Being initiated into the right house is the most crucial part of this process. You need to be compatible with the spirits that you will be serving and who will be ultimately serving you as well. The Lwa will say whether you have been approved as a new member of a specific house or not. There are instances where the spirit of a particular home will lay claim to a person explicitly. The reading must still be performed even when this happens to ensure the best fit for both the Lwa and the initiate.

FIVE

First Steps in Haitian Vodou

Illuminations

Illuminations are the bread and butter for a person who follows, practices and believes in the Vodou religion. Illuminations are the ways that we attract spirits and gain their attention to have them listen to our wants and needs. Illuminations may be spelled in many variations, but the most common is "illuminasyion." This is a powerful magic performance and can burn very hot. Typically, you would burn seven cotton wicks all at once in unison so that the spirits have a good and solid foundation to work with. Like the rites, there are many different variations of illuminations as well.

First, there is the illumination milocan. This illumination is done for all the spirits of a person to come forth during their escort. For those who need assistance and guidance and want all of their Lwa to help guide them, this is the best ceremony for them to perform. You prepare the cotton wicks and set them on top of a veve of milocan to call the spirits of your escort. You need to personally call them, then heat the cotton wicks and invite them to work on your problems for which you are seeking guidance.

You need a Houngan for this, and please do not attempt to

do it without one. Your Houngan will trace the veve and give introductory prayers and songs for the spirits. The cotton wicks will need to be adequately prepared and placed on a plate of oils. The plate the wicks are on will get put on a large enamel vessel and then filled with water. This is what you will present to your Lwa in prayer and set atop the veve. Burn it until it is completely burned out.

There is also the illumination Petro. It is close to the previous illumination milocan but aligned with the Petro rite. This illumination will burn hotter, faster, and much stronger than the first illumination we discussed. Even though the name is illumination Petro, this illumination can be used by all the rites of the Lwa—that includes the Rada, Nago, Petro, and Ghede as well.

You will follow the same movements you used for the illumination milocan, except you will not place water on the cavet. This removes the cooling of the ceremony, and your spirits will be heated faster, therefore, accomplishing your goal a lot faster too. Once the work is done, and your issues are solved, you do need to offer the spirits a cooling down service.

The main difference between the illumination petro and the illumination milocan is that in the petro illumination, you will not put the plate with the cotton wicks inside the cavet that is filled with water. You will simply place the plate on the veve that is ready and sing the songs of illumination. Then, as previous, you would leave the illumination to burn out completely while you pray over it.

Illumination Lwa yo is another final illumination that you present to only one single spirit. It is not as common that this illumination is used because most people want more Lwa to help them when they are facing hard decisions or troubles. You will have the Houngan prepare the veve for the specific Lwa that you wish to contact, and once you sing the songs of Legba, you will then sing for the Lwa to come forth to you. It does not matter too much which style you prepare the illumination in;

either the petro or milocan is fine. It must only suit your needs and the spirit which you are trying to make an agreement with. Sometimes this illumination can culminate in a spirit taking possession, but it does not always happen.

Actions De Grace

Actions of Grace is a ceremony in which an offering is presented to a Lwa as a way of giving thanks and gratitude. This follows typically when a Lwa has fulfilled or completed a request that was made of them. You need to do this to show your Lwa the gratitude for the work that they have done in your life. Sometimes you might want to offer up a ceremony of actions of grace just to show thankfulness at a momentous occasion being fulfilled, such as the birth of a child or a wedding.

You can offer this to one spirit in particular, or you can provide action for grace ceremony to many Lwa at once. This ceremony is a beautiful one in which people are often moved by how much the Lwa do for them. It is considered an act of grace in which the Lwa are invited to continue blessing their servers.

The Lave Tet

The Lave Tet is a necessary ceremony that all initiates need to go through as they begin their journey into Haitian Vodou. The purpose of the Lave Tet is to join a person with their house and also bring them closer in their relationship to the Lwa. This ceremony is supposed to serve to clean a person's mind and offer them a cool place to think from. This ceremony will elevate a person to the rank of "hounsi senp" in their house. Their spiritual escort will also be shown, and the initiate will be taught the methods to care for and respect the spirits that they walk with. During this ceremony, once all this is revealed, the initiate will be baptized with their spiritual Vodou name.

The head or mind is often significant in Vodou religion; therefore, it is cared for with devotion. The reason for this is because those that practice Vodou believe that the soul is within the head. So, a Vodou follower should always want to maintain a cool head and not get unbalanced or hot. When the head is cool, the spirit is calm and balanced, and the person receives the most from their connection to God and the Lwa. If you are naturally hot-headed, it can become hard to communicate with your Lwa and even God. Their luck will not often be good because they will be ruled by anger, and you cannot live in anger when you are trying to make offerings and blessings to the Lwa.

This is why the lave tet ceremony is so essential since it cools down the initiates head and allows them to think clearly and be balanced. A hot-headed initiate really benefits because this ceremony offers them a cool head; therefore, it will enable them to fully accept and embrace the blessings and communications from the spirit. If you have negative spirits that are influencing you in your path, the lave tet will clear these away as well. The whole purpose of the lave tet is to foster a closer relationship between the initiate and their Lwa.

The other important part of the lave tet ceremonies is that they also show who the Lwa Met Tet is going to be. The Lwa Met Tet is the Lwa that is master of the head. This means the spirit who will be walking most closely with the initiate. This Lwa that is revealed during this ceremony will forever stay with the initiate and it also helps place the initiate in their house. The relationship between this Lwa and the initiate should only grow with time.

Once the Lwa Met Tet is determined, there will be a ceremony made to the spirits, and the lave tet truly begins. This ceremony takes place in a room called a djevo (this simply means a place where initiations happen). The initiates are all given baths, and the details of the ceremony remain between the spirits and only those who are present.

Each initiate will leave the djevo as part of a procession. Once the initiates are clear of the djevo, they are then baptized and considered part of the house. The celebration will then begin to welcome the new member of the house.

The Garde (Gad)

A Gad or Garde is just what the name sounds like. It is

considered to be a guard to protect the person or even a place from any physical or spiritual harm. The guard will become a part of the person or situation that needs protection, and wherever the person or place is moved to, the guard will go too.

There are many types of gads that you can place all around yourself or a specific place. It is not a simple ceremony to accomplish, and it often takes hours to complete creating a gad. While you create and place a gad, you need to sing songs to grab the attention of Lwa and call them to you. A secret ceremony must be performed to put the gad down, and partakers of the ceremony swear an oath to keep the entire service a secret from anyone who was not present. You cannot just leave a gad once it is placed, all the same, as it must still be looked after. Every now and then you will want to use a Houngan or mambo to help you strengthen the protection upon the gad.

Gad Gilette is a ceremony in which a cut is made into your skin and sacred ingredients used for protection are rubbed into them.

Gad pwen is another type of protection that is laid onto a Lwa who is set to protect you.

Gads can also be placed on buildings or homes and even places of work to protect the premises from being harmed. This includes any spiritual or physical harm. The gads are generally placed in buildings that are being constructed and then worked into the building's frame, but they can also be placed in buildings that are already standing.

The Maryaj Lwa

This is a ceremony that we discussed earlier, the marriage to a Lwa. The Maryaj Lwa is a ceremony that a Houngan or Mambo will need to complete for you. The ceremony weds the participant to a specific Lwa. Usually, the Lwa will be called before the Maryaj Lwa takes place. The Lwa has the right to ask the human for their hand in marriage. For example, Ezili Danto often marries women, while Ezili Freda marries many men in her house. There are also Lwa who marry both male and female spouses. Some homes have rules in Vodou about the marriage to a Lwa and who a Lwa can rightfully marry.

You might be questioning why a person would wish to marry a Lwa. The answer to this question is a simple one:

- The Lwa offers the spouse health, good luck, protection, blessings, and unconditional support.
- The human might want to make a deeper connection with their Lwa, and by marrying their Lwa, they are strengthening their bonds with the Lwa. Sometimes it is because the Lwa demands the marriage.
- If a person does not want to go through Kanzo, which is an initiation process, then they may choose to marry a Lwa.
- If the human spouse has promised to the Lwa that they will.
- If the Lwa and the human entered into a contract for specific work to be done.
- If the human spouse never wants to be obligated to a person, but rather the spirits.
- If the person wants to work one-on-one with the Lwa in a capacity, other relationships do not provide.
- Marriage to the Lwa is much cheaper than performing the Kanzo ceremony.
- If the Lwa has communicated through dreams that their desire is to get married.

While these reasons do exist to enter into marriage with the Lwa spirits, there are also reasons why people do not want to marry Lwa:

- There is a restriction on their sexual activity. The human spouse must sleep alone and abstain for two days in every week as their commitment to their

Lwa. During those nights, the Lwa will visit their spouse in their dreams.
- This is a lifetime commitment. You can never divorce a Lwa once you are married to them.

The ceremony is conducted the exact same way a wedding would take place in a Roman Catholic Church. After it is done, there is a big reception that is prepared filled with the Lwa favorite items and food. The spouse will be allowed time to speak to their new Lwa spouse as a Houngan or Mambo helps guide the conversation.

Kanzo

Kanzo is the process where a Vodou initiation takes place. It does not matter what rank the person is when they initiate; the Kanzo ceremony is mandatory for them to ascend higher than the Hounsi senp status. The Kanzo ceremony is a solemn decision since it means that you enter into a lifetime commitment with God, the Lwa, and with the family that helps the initiate with their Kanzo ceremony.

Even though you might complete the Kanzo ceremony, this does not mean that you are going to be called to the priesthood. Everyone has their place. Some will serve their house, and others will take up higher positions. Some even go through Kanzo so that they can be healed. Sometimes the Lwa will call initiates to the priesthood, but your Lwa will determine what role you play in your house.

Kanzo is more than one ceremony, but rather a series of many services that take place for three weeks. These ceremonies are supposed to empower those who partake in them the rank that they will take up in their house. When they have completed Kanzo, they are considered strong and competent members of their home.

Wanga

Wanga is a highly requested ceremony, and most Houngans and Mambos find themselves performing many wanga ceremonies. The wanga is technically considered a spell, and like other aspects of Vodou, there is more than one type of wanga and more than one way to build a wanga.

Wanga can take the form of secrets that a Houngan or mambo know; other wanga can be traditional spells. The traditional Wanga is commonly known by most Houngans and Mambos. When a wanga is done, they say that a Houngan or mambo has "tied a wanga." Still, not all wanga are tied. This is because you have those who are uninitiated in the Vodou religion who try to perform magick—wanga being amongst this magic. Because of their close relationship to the Lwa in the Vodou religion, the Houngans and Mambos have greater leverage when completing Wangas to solve their client's issues. By going through a Kanzo ceremony, the Houngans and Mambos have greater clarity when tying a wanga.

When it comes to magick, both Houngans and Mambos have a full set of Wangas they can use to help out with problems. There are times where the client with a problem does need to do some of the work on their own, but mostly the Houngan or Mambo will elicit the help of the Lwa to help tie the magick together.

There are also different kinds of Wanga, as I mentioned above. There are wanga that are made to stop things, and they are classified as "aret." There are also wanga that are made to release things called "lage."

A Houngan or Mambo can create a pwen cho or even give the client a bath or powder that they need to spread. The wanga can also be released in a perfume that the client is told to wear. The premise of Vodou is that no problem does not have a solution. This is why Houngans and Mambos are so crucial because their knowledge helps provide answers to obstacles.

Wanga can be used to help a client gain strength with their psyche. It works by creating change in the client's life and empowers the client to take steps to make the changes they need to accomplish as well physically. Remember that while Houngans and Mambos can help with their magick and alleviate a lot of problems, they are not God or spirits like the Lwa. Usually, it takes wanga about one month to be constructed and to begin working. Sometimes this can be faster, and sometimes it can take longer.

SIX

Magic and Sorcery

The Societies of Sorcerers

Houngans and Mambos are the priests and priestesses of the Vodou religion. The dead ancestors were the ones who chose them to receive initiation and become a Houngan or Mambo. They are supposed to do good deeds for their people; their job is to help and protect their people. There are times where a Houngan or Mambo might use their powers and abilities to kill or harm a person, but this is not the standard for which they practice. They conduct ceremonies frequently underneath Vodou temples and are supposed to be leaders for their people.

The society of sorcerers is merely the network that revolved around protecting Haiti's Vodou culture, rituals, and ceremonies. For example, there are clergy who exist in the Haitian Vodou religion whose only responsibility is to protect and preserve the rituals that are used to maintain and keep up the Lwa's relationship with the humans.

There is a tool called the calabash rattle, which is used as a symbol to show those who have earned the status of priest or priestess in the Vodou realm. The calabash rattle is formed from the bark of a tree that holds cultural significance to the Vodou religion.

A bokor in the Vodou realm is considered a direct sorcerer or even a magician. They cast spells as they are requested of them, but they might not be priests or priestesses. Typically, a bokor will take their magic into darker places, and this is not accepted by the Mambo or Houngan in Vodou. A bokor is considered a sorcerer or magician. This sorcerer is known to cast spells for people who request them too, regardless of intent. Bokors are not really priests or priestesses, but rather, they practice dark magic. Because of the sinister nature of their magic, Bokors are not often accepted by the Mambo or Houngan.

White Magic

There is an ideology that exists that the universe is filled with intelligent and intuitive power. The idea of white magic is the notion that this power can be influenced by humans, and we can control the flow of white magic.

They believe that everything in this world is connected on some level, in a network of power that flows from one object to the next. In fact, when we see a hidden object, the truth is that with the knowledge behind white power, we are aware that that object that first appears isolated in fact connected to everything around it. When it is changed, other objects around it are influenced.

This is how the magic in Vodou works. It is considered white magic, not black magic. All that the Houngans and Mambos are doing is to control the flow of that supernatural power with the help of their Lwa spirit guides.

Divination

Divination plays one of the most critical roles in Vodou. In fact, it is known as the top sought after service that a Houngan or Mambo can perform. Most Haitian Vodou divination uses playing cards. These are used to obtain and give a reading. What the Houngan or Mambo will do during this type of prophecy to invoke a spirit of the Lwa to take possession and perform the divination. The purpose of divination is to allow the person to see what the problem is, find the root of the problem, identify the spirits involved with the problem, and then work to find a solution. Sounds simple enough, right?

But that is not the only way that divination happens. In fact, sometimes the readings performed are called lessons because the person receiving the reading will receive a lesson rather than a simple solution to the problem.

Most Houngan and Mambo who call on Lwa to take possession for divinations will have a relationship with a particular Gede Lwa or even at times an Ogou Lwa. They are the best spirits to use for divination because of their ability at foresight. Not all divinations need cards, though. Some Houngan and Mambos might choose to use a candle and a glass of water.

Divination is generally done before wanga is performed so that the Houngan or Mambo can make sure that they are going the best route to solve their client's problem. The other reason divination is so popular is that it is one of the least expensive choices when it comes to seeking the help of a Houngan or Mambo.

Conclusion

Congratulations!! You have reached the end of the book, and by now you should have an in-depth understanding of not just what Haitian Vodou is, but also how Haiti's history has been shaped by the use of Haitian Vodou. I encourage you to continue learning and expand more of your knowledge about this world of Vodou. Better yet, share what you have learned with someone else so that they too can be introduced to the beautiful and complicated world of Haitian Vodou.

Vodou is about more than just spirits and magic. It is a religion that is based on community and communication with our ancestors and God. There is nothing evil or harmful about Vodou when it is used and wielded the right way.

If you find that you are still called to learn more about Vodou, I urge you to reach out to a Houngan or Mambo so that they can help guide you in the right direction. The history from Haiti is indeed tragic, but amongst all, that tragedy is the rise of a religion that has unified an entire country, boosted the tourist economy, and provided those alive a deeper connection with God and their ancestors. I wish you luck on your journey into the world of Vodou!

Glossary

A

Adjessi: Wife to Legba.

Agwe: Lwa who rules over the sea, fish, and aquatic plants. Especially in Haiti, he is patron Lwa of fishermen and sailors in Vodou. Agwe is considered to be married to Erzulie Freda and La Sirene.

Ancestors: Those who have gone before.

Ayizan: A Lwa of the commerce and business in Vodou.

B

Baron Cimitiere: One of the intensely powerful Lwa of the Dead.

Bokor: Also known as a Boko is a sorcerer who conducts Spiritual work for patrons in return for favors or money. What singles them out from other practitioners is a Bokor work using both hands. Accurately, they will conduct various rituals involving black magick and will-control that the majority of other-initiated Vodou practitioners will not.

Bossou: The spirit of the deceased Dahomean King Tegbessou in Haiti. As the manifestation of the Petro, Bossou is frequently portrayed as a horned bull.

Glossary

Boukman: A Houngan who assembled secret Vodou ceremonies and meetings set in motion the Haitian Revolution.

C

Creole: About the customs, people, and language of Haiti.

D

Damballah: The principal Sky-Serpent Lwa of Vodou.

Djabs: A tremendous but wild spirit having both good and bad potential.

Djakout: A hand-woven straw sack with tassel ornament, used in serving different Lwa or to carry Vodou tools.

E

Ezili Danto: A Haitian Vodou Petro Lwa. Ezili Dantor is one of the most celebrated female Petro Lwa.

Ezili Freda: As an extraordinarily magickal and beautiful Lwa, She is the Queen of Love, beauty, romance, and riches.

F

Filomez: A Lwa that belongs to the Rada nation. She is a water spirit.

G

Ghede: The most generous of the Lwa of the Dead. Ghede is powerful in healing and as the guardian of children.

Gran Ibo: The Haitian goddess of wisdom and patience. She is seen as the great mistress, the grandmother, the wise old woman of the swamp.

Grand Bwa: King of the Ancestral Forests Gran Bwa is invoked to protect animals and keep safe, healing, keeping secrets, trees, and wilderness, increasing finances.

H

Hoodoo: An African-American tradition of folk magic, herbal medicine, and conjuring, which is not related to Vodou. Hoodoo is neither a religion nor a classification of a religion.

Hounfor: The inner sanctum or altar room of a place where the religion of Vodou is performed.

Houngan: A fully initiated priest of Vodoun who has accepted the Asson.

Glossary

Hounsi: An accepted follower at a Hounfor. Those not adequately trained, and consequently directed with the more ordinary duties, are called hounsis bossale.

Hounsi Kanzo: An initiate of the Vodou who has experienced the ritual of Kanzo.

K

Kalfou: A Petro Lwa of the crossroads or Gate between the Worlds.

Kanzo: The initiation ceremony for individuals advancing into a very dangerous level of Vodou custom. This is very secret service.

Kouzen Zaka: The farming spirits of Haiti.

Kreyol: The language of Haiti.

L

Lave Tet: A ceremonial head washing to cleanse the head spiritually.

Legba: The most potent Lwa, Legba safeguards the gateway connecting the material and spiritual worlds.

Loko: The spirit of vegetation and protector of sanctuaries. Chiefly connected with trees.

Lwa: The Lwa are the spirits of Vodou. An African word, it is both singular and plural. While the modern Haitian Kreyol spelling is Lwa, the French spelling is Loa. Lwa is also referred to as mystères and the invisibles.

M

François Makandal: A one-armed, Boko, revolutionary hero and prophet who taught poisoning as a method of effective protection in the mid-1700s.

Maman Brigitte: The female Guardian of Graves. Maman Brigitte is a powerful magical Lwa of cemeteries.

Mambo: A Vodoun priestess who has taken the same instruction as a Houngan and in the same way has received the Asson.

Marassa: The divine twins in Vodou. Although they are children, Marassa is more ancient than any other Lwa.

Glossary

Met Kay: A Lwa who is the head or leader of a Vodou temple.

Met Tet: The Lwa who controls the initiates head. This is comparable to what some would acknowledge as a Guardian Angel.

N

Nago: A custom, rhythm dance of Lwa. Foremost among these is Ogou.

O

Ogou: Primarily a warrior-Lwa, he carries all the associations of Mars.

Oungan: A fully initiated priest of Vodou.

P

Papa Doc: François Duvalier, former president of Haiti, whose 14-year rule was of unparalleled extent in that country. Papa Doc imposed a dynasty of intimidation on a nation. His secret police, the Tontons Macoutes, which happens to be Creole for bogeymen, executed and tortured his adversaries, frequently leaving behind a victim's detached head on exhibit in a marketplace as an example to others.

Peristyle: A great deck or more or less open-sided building adjoining to the altar room of a hounfort.

Poteau-mitan: The central post of the peristyle, the place about which most public services of Vodoun revolve.

Petro Lwa: Some of the most famous Lwa around the world, Petro Lwa are generally regarded to be angry or demon Lwa, used in black magic.

R

Rada Lwa: A notable family of Lwa in Haitian Vodou which includes older, benevolent spirits.

S

Saint Domingue: The French colony on the Caribbean isle of Hispaniola from 1659 to 1804, in what is now known as Haiti.

Glossary

Simbi: The magical and powerful Water-Snake Lwa, who is served with Rada as well as Petro rites.

T

Taking of the Asson: The last initiation into being a Houngan or Mambo. This is a very secret service.

V

Vincent Ogé: A member of the free colored planter class in Saint-Domingue. He instigated a rebellion against white colonial rule in French Saint-Domingue.

Vodou: A creolized faith built by descendants of Kongo, Dahomean, Yoruba, and additional African ethnic groups which had been captured and transported to colonial Saint-Domingue, which Haiti was recognized as then.

W

Wanga: A magical charm packet found in the folk magic works of Haiti.

About the Author

Monique Joiner Siedlak is a writer, witch, and warrior on a mission to awaken people to their greatest potential through the power of storytelling infused with mysticism, modern paganism, and new age spirituality. At the young age of 12, she began rigorously studying the fascinating philosophy of Wicca. By the time she was 20, she was self-initiated into the craft, and hasn't looked back ever since. To this day, she has authored over 40 books pertaining to the magick and mysteries of life.

To find out more about Monique Joiner Siedlak artistically, spiritually, and personally, feel free to visit her **official website**.

www.mojosiedlak.com

facebook.com/mojosiedlak
twitter.com/mojosiedlak
instagram.com/mojosiedlak
pinterest.com/mojosiedlak
bookbub.com/authors/monique-joiner-siedlak

More Books by Monique Joiner Siedlak

Practical Magick

Wiccan Basics

Candle Magick

Wiccan Spells

Love Spells

Abundance Spells

Herb Magick

Moon Magick

Creating Your Own Spells

Gypsy Magic

Personal Growth and Development

Creative Visualization

Astral Projection for Beginners

Meditation for Beginners

Reiki for Beginners

Manifesting With the Law of Attraction

Stress Management

The Yoga Collective

Yoga for Beginners

Yoga for Stress

Yoga for Back Pain

Yoga for Weight Loss

Yoga for Flexibility

Yoga for Advanced Beginners

Yoga for Fitness

Yoga for Runners

Yoga for Energy

Yoga for Your Sex Life

Yoga to Beat Depression and Anxiety

Yoga for Menstruation

Yoga to Detox Your Body

Yoga to Tone Your Body

A Natural Beautiful You

Creating Your Own Body Butter

Creating Your Own Body Scrub

Creating Your Own Body Spray

THANK YOU FOR READING MY BOOK! I REALLY APPRECIATE ALL OF YOUR FEEDBACK AND I LOVE TO HEAR WHAT YOU HAVE TO SAY. PLEASE LEAVE YOUR REVIEW AT YOUR FAVORITE RETAILER!

www.ingramcontent.com/pod-product-compliance
Lightning Source LLC
Chambersburg PA
CBHW071620040426
42452CB00009B/1408